The Family Circus Album

By Bil Keane

FAWCETT COLUMBINE · NEW YORK

A Fawcett Columbine Book
Published by Ballantine Books
Copyright © 1984 by The Register and Tribune Syndicate, Inc.

All Family Circus materials copyright © 1960–1984 by the
Register and Tribune Syndicate, Inc.

Foreword copyright ©1984 by Charles M. Schulz

All rights reserved under International and Pan-American
Copyright Conventions. Published in the United States by
Ballantine Books, a division of Random House, Inc.,
New York, and simultaneously in Canada by Random
House of Canada Limited, Toronto.

Library of Congress Catalog Card Number: 84-90843

ISBN 0-449-90098-3

Manufactured in the United States of America

Designed by Gene Siegel

First Edition: November 1984

10   9   8   7   6   5   4   3   2   1

*To my wife Thel, without whose loving help
our real-life "Family Circus," and consequently
this 25th Anniversary Album, could not have
been produced.*

"I like reading. It turns on pictures in your head."

FOREWORD

It is impossible, if not also desirable, to create a daily comic feature for twenty-five years without at least a portion of your own personality creeping in. I believe that if you know the family and other characters of "The Family Circus," you can be quite assured that you also know Bil Keane—which means you know a lot of nice people.

"Niceness" is not so easy. Readers are prone to complain that there should be more happy things in our cartoons, but happiness is just about as funny as niceness. This is where Bil triumphs. We are surrounded in all mediums by ugliness, and yet, Bil has been able to entertain millions of readers every day and remain at the top of his profession by drawing characters who are decent people.

We are fortunate, as human beings, that we can laugh at all the strange things that happen to us, and even though we seem to be living on the brink of disaster, we are blessed with the ability to laugh together as we battle fear, loneliness, illness and all those other terrible things that leap out at us every day. Bil can take all of these things, give them to his characters to wrestle with, and make us laugh and understand. The characters in "Family Circus" love each other, and because they do, we do also.

There is nothing wrong with niceness.

Charles M. Schulz

I couldn't have hired a better cast of cartoon models than the five little Keanes shown here in 1958: Jeff, Chris, Glen, Neal, and Gayle.

INTRODUCTION

By Bil Keane

This "Album" consists of a selection of the cartoons I have drawn and a cross section of the family snapshots I have taken or posed for through the years. It is hard to say which are funnier—the cartoons or the photos.

I have also included a running commentary (that's how I do most of my commentaries—running) about behind-the-scenes incidents connected with some of the daily panels and Sunday pages.

As you might imagine, we receive a flood of mail from our readers. Well, not exactly a flood, but certainly a flow of letters that—anyhow, a postcard trickles in every so often. Some of the reader comment is scattered throughout the book.

I hope some of your favorite cartoons are reprinted here. I have been asked which is my favorite. It is usually the one I thought of last night and am about to draw today.

MY OTHER RIGHT HAND

Bud Warner, a fantastic all-around artist, has been my assistant since 1965. He works in Phoenix in his own studio and is responsible for the inking of my cartoons. To him goes credit for the very flattering things which have been said about the "Family Circus" finished art, most of which have been said by Bud Warner. It is a delight to work with such a fine gentleman, even though he is quite elderly. He was born five days before me.

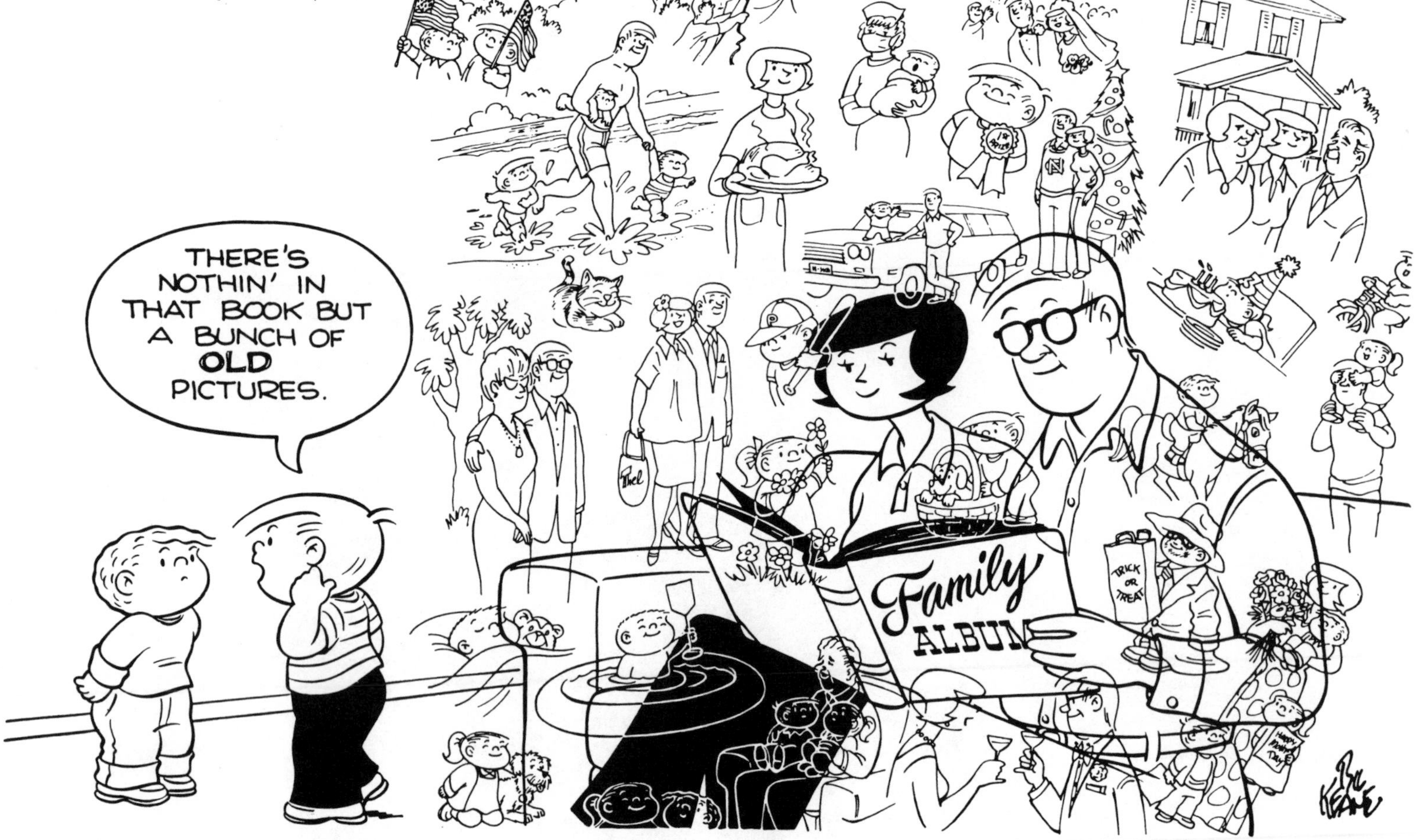
THERE'S NOTHIN' IN THAT BOOK BUT A BUNCH OF **OLD** PICTURES.
Family ALBUM
TRICK OR TREAT

1953 in Roslyn, PA, at my home drawing board when the ideas for "Family Circus" were happening every day, but I hadn't yet thought of the feature. Things are funnier in retrospect. At this time I was working as a staff artist at the Philadelphia Bulletin which has since ceased publication. I was also contributing free-lance cartoons to Colliers, The Saturday Evening Post, Look, This Week—all the magazines I drew for have folded.

With all this help, how could "Family Circus" miss? I submitted all my cartoons for my wife Thel's approval before mailing them to the Syndicate—and still do. She has been my editor, adviser, model for "Mommy," and tennis partner all these years. The kids, before they grew up on us, also pitched in with criticisms and suggestions.

INTERVIEW WITH Bil Keane PART I

Q. Thank you for inviting me to the 25th Birthday party of the "Family Circus."

A. Did you bring me a present?

Q. Not exactly, Mr. Keane, but I...

A. Put on your paper party hat, and please call me Bil.

Q. Bil, why do you live out here in the Arizona desert?

A. To avoid interviews. But it doesn't work.

Q. Most people in Arizona have migrated here from someplace else. Have you lived here your whole life?

A. Not yet.

Q. Where did you come from?

A. Well, you see, the male sperm unites with the ovum and the...

Q. Just when did "Family Circus" start?

A. Eat your ice cream. The daily panel started on February 29th, 1960.

Q. And how long have you been drawing the Sunday page?

A. I've been drawing it about 26 inches long, but it's reduced for reproduction in the papers.

Q. Why is the daily panel drawn in a circle?

A. When I did the first one I reached for a ruler to put a border around it and picked up my compass by mistake.

Q. And you've been going in circles ever since.

A. On second thought, call me Mr. Keane.

Q. How many papers publish the feature?

A. Well, let's see. The *New York Daily News*, that's one; the *Los Angeles Times*, that's two. The *Philadelphia Inquirer* is three, the...

Q. This could take a long time. Don't you have over a thousand papers?

A. I'm counting. The *Washington Post* is four, the...

Q. Most cartoonists draw themselves to some extent. In "Peanuts" some say Charlie Brown is in reality Charles Schulz. Do you do that?

A. No, Schulz does it. I draw "The Family Circus."

Q. Is it difficult after all these years coming up with new ideas?

A. Frankly, it seems to get easier, It's…well, I find that it's…

Q. A piece of cake?

A. No, thanks. I had one right after I blew out the candles.

Q. Which character do you like to draw best?

A. Well, I like to draw Garfield, but I can't get the eyes right.

Q. Bil, let's get serious for a moment. You've been very fortunate in having a successful career surrounded by a fine family. Do you ever stop and count your blessings?

A. Certainly. The *Milwaukee Journal*, that's five…

Q. I understand you are putting together a book to celebrate your 25th year.

A. That's right: THE FAMILY CIRCUS ALBUM. It's being published by Fawcett Columbine, a fine publishing house.

Q. What does it consist of?

A. Oh, the usual. A few editors, the sales people, an art department…

Q. I hope I get a copy of it when it is released.

A. Look, why don't you give me your money now and I'll have it sent to you.

Q. Later. Somebody once said that the daily happenings in "Family Circus" reflect the American home life as accurately as a mirror.

A. Right. I'm the one who said it.

Q. The continuing feature is an on-going record, a part of the times.

A. The *Greensboro Record* that's six, *Seattle Times*, that's seven…

Q. Well, I guess the party's over. I'll leave now, but we'll continue this interview later.

A. Thanks for coming. Wait by the front door till your Mommy comes to pick you up.

THE CIRCUS COMES TO TOWN

In 1960, when the feature first appeared, my art was quite different. "Crude," "primitive," "unfinished" were some of the words used by critics. They were talking about ME! My drawings they liked.

"And in here is the children's playroom."

"It's for our mother and here's her charge plate."

"The cavemen let their kids do it!"

"Daddy takes off weight by turning this little wheel!"

The characters had a slightly different appearance then. My style was more "cartoony." But close followers of the feature have said the ideas and situations were the same as I am drawing today and why don't I get some new gags?

"We're just one shoe away from leaving."

"Daddy, have you talked to Mr. Horton about the raise yet?"

I caricatured the late Bruce Horton, at that time President of the Register and Tribune Syndicate, which distributes my cartoons. I still draw him as Daddy's boss.

"Instead of a couple regular aspirin, Bruce, how about eight orange flavored ones?"

"How's it taste? I made it out of play dough!"

"I thought Halloween came in October."

"Petersons have our bassinet. Thirkhills
borrowed the coach, we can get our
high chair back from the Hulls..."

"Where in Heaven do ya hail from, stranger?"

In 1962 I depicted Mommy wearing mater-
nity clothes and on August 1st that year PJ
was born into the feature. Till that time only
three children were in the cartoon family:
Billy, Dolly, and Jeffy. Jeffy didn't like the
addition very much.

"Mommy loves me...she loves me not..."

"Keep rattling! He'll go back to sleep soon."

"Suppose a mother bird sees him."

"I'd like to exchange these pink things for blue ones."

4-3
Copyright 1969
The Register and Tribune
Syndicate, Inc.

"In school today we learned how to loot the flag
and take the pledge."

6-15
Copyright 1963
The Register and Tribune
Syndicate, Inc.

"Good night, sleep tight, don't let the bed bugs bite!"

*Not only did I draw the characters from real life, I
even drew furniture and props from around the
home. This rocking chair served as the inspiration for
the drawing on the opposite page.*

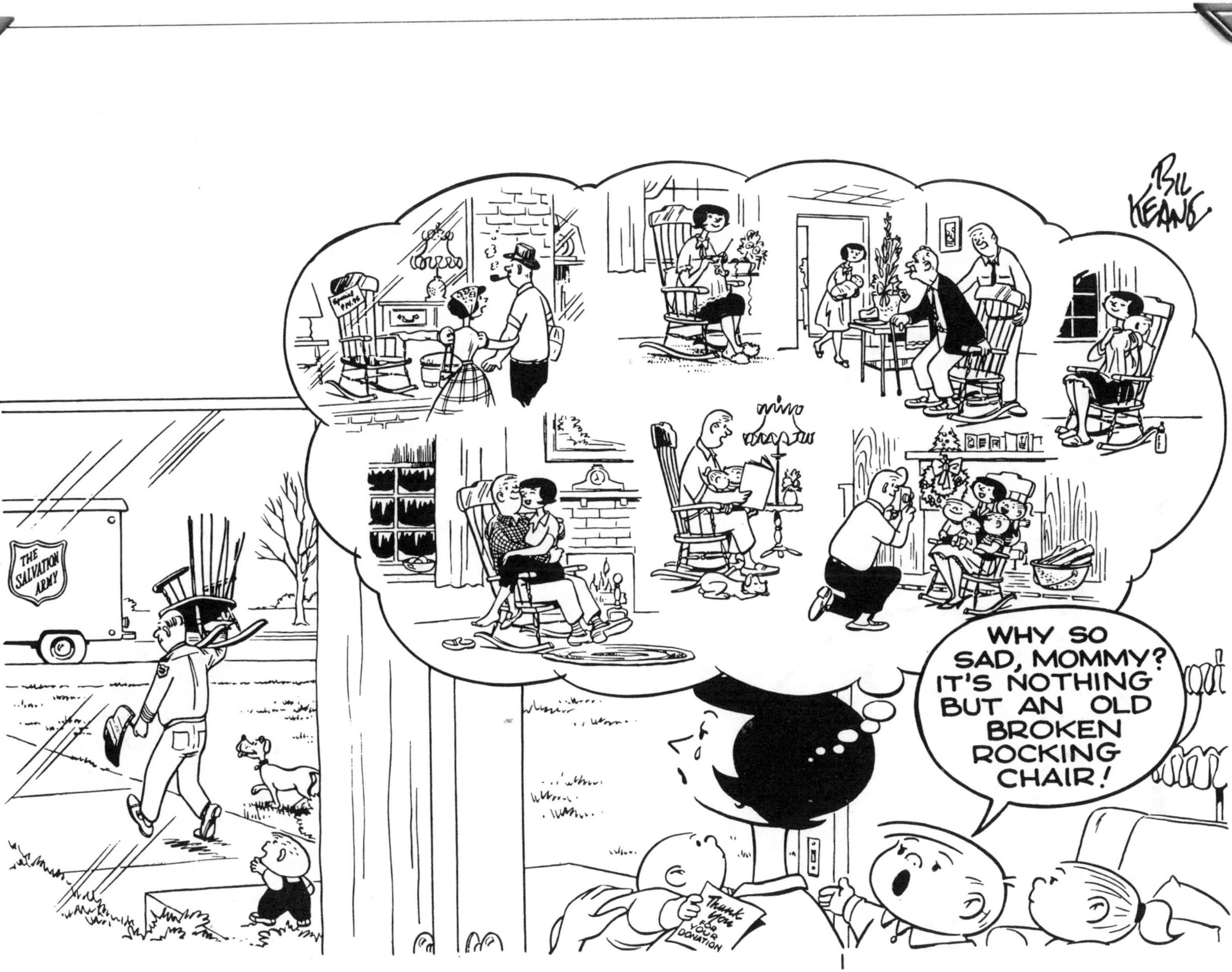
BIL KEANE
THE SALVATION ARMY
WHY SO SAD, MOMMY? IT'S NOTHING BUT AN OLD BROKEN ROCKING CHAIR!
Thank You FOR YOUR DONATION

8-16

"Shall I bring PJ out? He's just wasting those pretty smiles in here all by himself."

3-1

"Glad we have this drawer—You never know when we'll need a broken pencil, a plastic car wheel, a bottle cap, half a scissors, a doll's arm..."

10-19

FORMER
PHILA. BULLETIN
NEWSPAPERBOY

"Mommy! 'Collect' is here!"

I usually saluted the newspaper carriers of the nation on National Newspaperboy Day. I have a special affinity for these guys and gals as this was my introduction to the newspaper business in Crescentville, PA (a suburb of Philadelphia, PA) in 1934. The *Ledger* folded (naturally) and I later delivered the *Philadelphia Bulletin.*

PJ was quite bald for the first few years he appeared. Finally he grew hair and even learned to walk. However, he now remains at 18 months of age. Jeffy is 3 years, Dolly 5, and Billy an ancient 7.

7-12

"It's a lucky thing PJ's still in diapers while he's learning to walk—he needs the padding."

3-20

"Can I use your comb and brush, Mommy? PJ's growing hair!"

5-8

"He has some teeth, but his words haven't come in yet."

Ideas unfolded every day on the back lawn just outside my studio. I simply had to observe and draw them into a cartoon.

6-12

"Aw, go on, PJ! What are you—a BABY?"

6-13

"I'm here, PJ! I'll catch you!"

Barfy was the only animal in "The Family Circus" until one winter day in 1970 when a stray dog became a permanent member of the cast. The kids named him Sam. A stray cat wandered into our home and modeled for Kittycat.

"Well, all right. We'll keep him 'til we find out who his owner is."

"...And he's very shaggy and wearing no collar. If you've lost this dog please phone us as the people who found him are anxious to find its owner."

"Mommy! That kitty-cat got into our house!"

"The difference between dogs and cats is cats like to THINK about what they're going to do."

"That's okay. Cats are allowed up on things but dogs aren't."

"We should be very kind to cats and dogs because they have no words."

The real life Sam and Kittycat.

HO! HO! HO!
IT'S CHRISTMAS!

Every year Christmas provides "The Family Circus" with a seasonal series that many readers look forward to. On the following pages are a few of my favorite yuletide cartoons that have appeared. I particularly like to draw Santa Claus, toys, tree decorations, gifts, etc., because I am just a kid at heart.

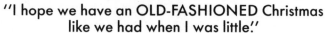

"I hope we have an OLD-FASHIONED Christmas like we had when I was little."

"What I DON'T want is clothes."

"Stop it, PJ. Don't you know this is the season
to be jolly?"

"If you get caught under that mistletoe you
hafta get kissed."

"Let's get one that's real wide at the bottom so
there'll be room for lots of presents."

"On, Comet! On, Cupid! On, Donder and Blitzen!"

"It'll look a lot happier once it's wearin' all its lights and stuff!"

"My brother is one of the wise guys!"

"Dear Santa, bless Mommy and Daddy and ...I mean, Dear God, bless Mommy and..."

12-15

Copyright 1979
The Register and Tribune
Syndicate, Inc.

"Mmm! Now the house is beginnin' to SMELL like Christmas!"

12-8

Copyright 1980
The Register and Tribune
Syndicate, Inc.

"And Joseph couldn't get them a room 'cause all the motels were overbooked."

12-18

Copyright 1980
The Register and Tribune
Syndicate, Inc.

"But I don't wanna just hand it to you, Daddy. I wanna climb up and hang it myself."

12-19

Copyright 1979
The Register and Tribune
Syndicate, Inc.

"Sun's set! Can we turn the tree on now?"

12-24

"Don't you hafta go up on the roof to hang
them by the chimney with care?"

Bil, Gayle, Glen, and Neal. Christmas, 1954.

12-17

"We can't play now. We hafta help our daddy
put up the Christmas lights."

12-27

"Mommy! Jeffy's bein' like Scrooge!"

"I had Mommy's wrapped at the store, but I did Daddy's myself."

"Should I say, 'Dear Santa', or 'Dear Mr. Claus'?"

"Let's tell each other what we want for Christmas."

"The child is three and the father is not mechanically inclined."

12-19

"It's the best tree we've ever had!"
"Aw, Mommy, you say that every year."

12-23

"When they're finished singin', do we just
smile or clap or what?"

12-17

"We've watched enough Christmas specials for
tonight, Mommy. Guess we'll brush
our teeth and go to bed."

12-23

"...Holy instant so tender and mild..."

OUR COLORFUL LIFE

Jeff and Chris, 1963.

Chris and Jeff toasting marshmallows.

Bathtime, 1950.

DON'T COME IN HERE, MOMMY! I DON'T HAVE ANY CLOTHES ON!
BIL KEANE
2-6

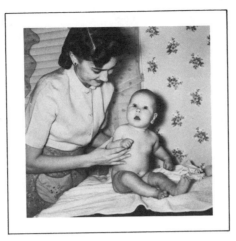

Jeff, 1962.

I drew this from my own recollection as a child. Jeff (now a grown man and an actor in California) told me after seeing the cartoon, that it must have been drawn about him. Kids of every age are alike. And so are the parents.

3-5
Copyright 1978, The Register and Tribune Syndicate, Inc

Thel talking with her family on her birthday, March 15, 1958. Philadelphia to Australia—now THAT'S long distance.

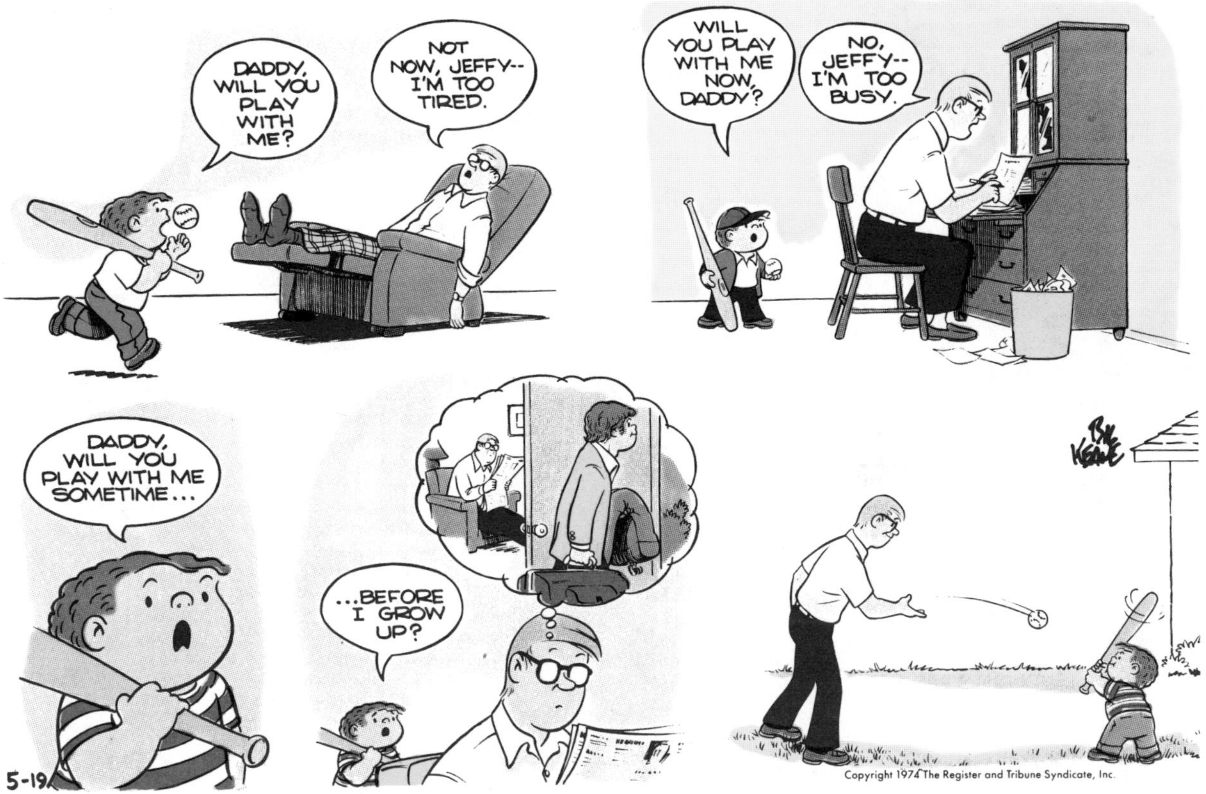
DADDY, WILL YOU PLAY WITH ME?
NOT NOW, JEFFY-- I'M TOO TIRED.
WILL YOU PLAY WITH ME NOW, DADDY?
NO, JEFFY-- I'M TOO BUSY.
DADDY, WILL YOU PLAY WITH ME SOMETIME...
...BEFORE I GROW UP?
BIL KEANE
5-19
Copyright 1974 The Register and Tribune Syndicate, Inc.

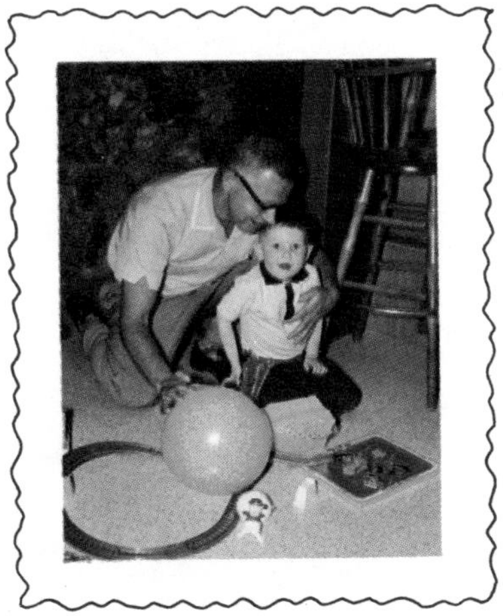

Bil playing with Jeff, 1961.

Dear Mr. Keane,
How did you see into our home last week? Our nine-year-old was sick in bed and you captured the entire scene, even to our youngest wanting to be the next guest of honor in the sickbed.
You draw our family so accurately, I am sure you are a peeping Tom.

Mrs. George K.
Baltimore, MD

Dear Mrs. K.,
You're close. I'm a peeping Bil. Thank you for writing.
Bil Keane

Some of the most difficult ideas to come up with are the ones for special days that come around every year. Providing a different variation on a similar theme every twelve months requires more effort than just an ordinary Sunday. Mother's Day is one of my favorite days, although Father's Day isn't bad either.

Dear Mr. Keane,
On behalf of all the lonely grandmothers in the country, let me thank you for graphically portraying an absolute truth. Oh, what a gloom-disperser that "Hi, Grandma" can be.
Mrs. Fran McG.
Houston, Texas

This was drawn shortly after Thel and I played in a local mixed-doubles tournament in Phoenix. However, I must confess Thel played a lot better than I. She concentrated and I did the woolgathering. After all, I was thinking of the idea for this cartoon.

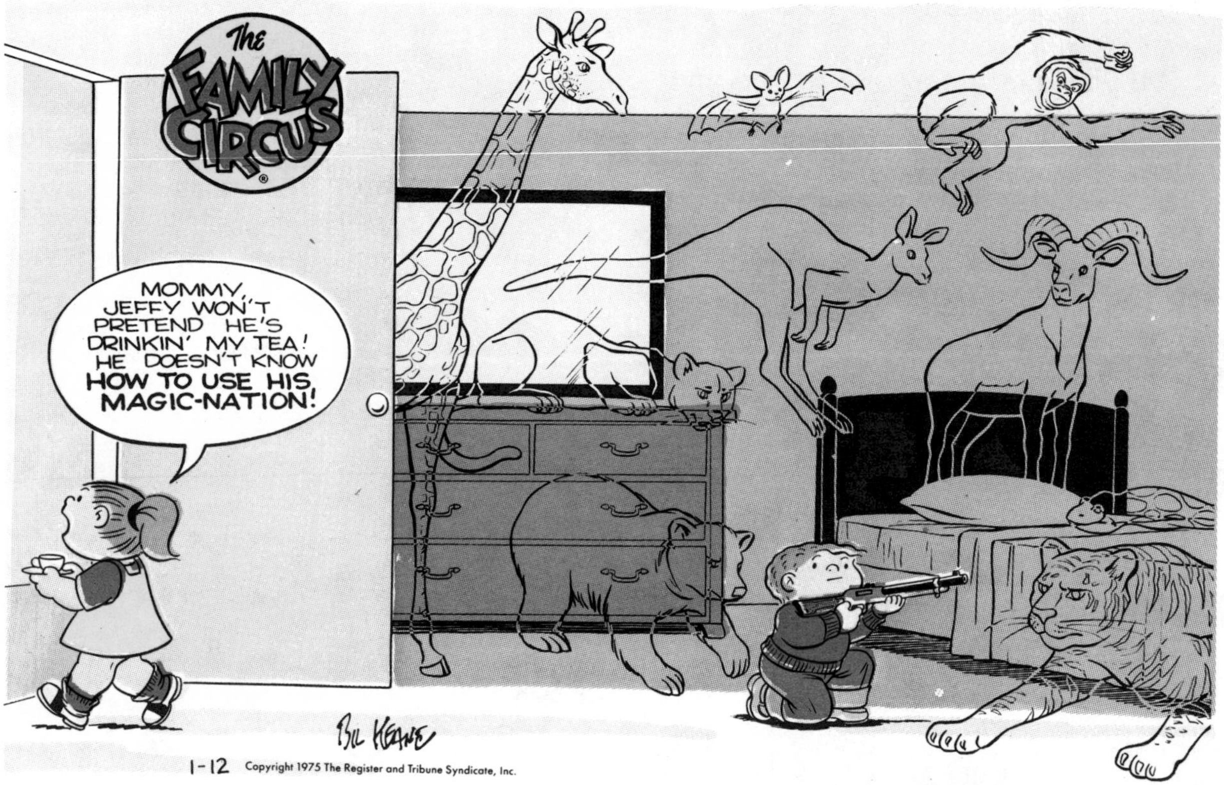
The FAMILY CIRCUS
MOMMY, JEFFY WON'T PRETEND HE'S DRINKIN' MY TEA! HE DOESN'T KNOW HOW TO USE HIS MAGIC-NATION!
BIL KEANE

1-12

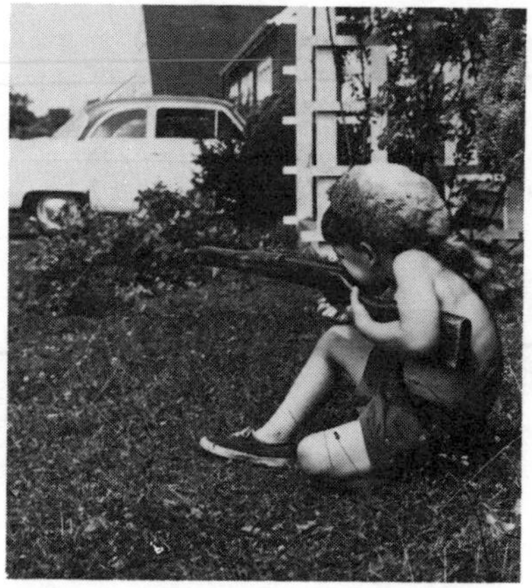

Neal, 1956.

WERE THE COMICS INVENTED YET WHEN YOU WERE A GIRL, GRANDMA?

INDEED THEY WERE, JEFFY.

6-1

BIL KEANE

When this cartoon appeared many comic buffs wrote for the identity of the various old-time characters Grandma is envisioning. I will include their names for your convenience: Upper left to right: Skippy, The Timid Soul, Little Nemo, Andy Gump, and Krazy Kat. Middle row: Skeezix (Gasoline Alley), Toots and Casper, Rudolph Rassendale (from Hairbreadth Harry), Paw (from Polly and Her Pals), and the Skipper (of the Toonerville Trolley). Bottom line: Barney Google, Jiggs (of Bringing Up Father), The Little King, Tillie the Toiler, and Happy Hooligan.

On most Father's Days Billy contributes a page of his own creation (see opposite page). Here I drew the cartoon using the multi-balloon format where all the kids' comments are presented in one scene. My wife insists these pages use up too many good lines. I feel there is safety in numbers. Somewhere among all these balloons there has to be one each reader will like.

Most readers assume these childish drawings are done by "young Billy." They are
really done by "old Daddy," struggling to
make the drawings and ideas appear to
have emanated from a seven-year-old. I
love the pun type humor and a couple of
our boys drew exactly like this when they
were seven.

Dear Billy,
   Your cartoons each Father's Day and every so often throughout the year are marvelous. They are my kind of jokes. Many tanks!
   Tell your daddy I will continue to read his comic, but yours are my favorites.
                              Mrs. Stanley S.
                              Wauwatosa, WI

Dear Little Billy,
   I know your father appreciates the help when you draw his Sunday cartoon for him, but I want you to know how much our whole family enjoys your efforts.
   Keep practicing and you, too, will be a successful artist some day.
                              The George T. Family
                              Wilkes Barre, PA

WHILE BIL KEANE ATTENDS THE NATIONAL CARTOONISTS SOCIETY'S GATHERING IN L.A., LITTLE BILLY FILLS IN WITH THIS PAGE FEATURING HIS OWN BRAND OF HUMOR.
MOMMY HELPED ME WITH SOME OF THE NAMES.
Map of Oh-Pun Country By Billy
Dinah's Shore
Christmas Reef
High Sea
Exclamation Point
Blindman's Bluff
Night Falls
Tension's mountain
Rudy Valley
Merry Isthmus
Steve Canyon
Veronica Lake
Contrail
Dudley Moor
Punk Rock
Tinker's Dam
Don't Peak
Root Canal
Jet Plains
Joan Rivers
Lorna Dunes
Hugh Downs
Decimal Point
Al Cove
Miniature Gulf
Superman Cape
Dire Straits
Isle of View
Can't Sea
4-17

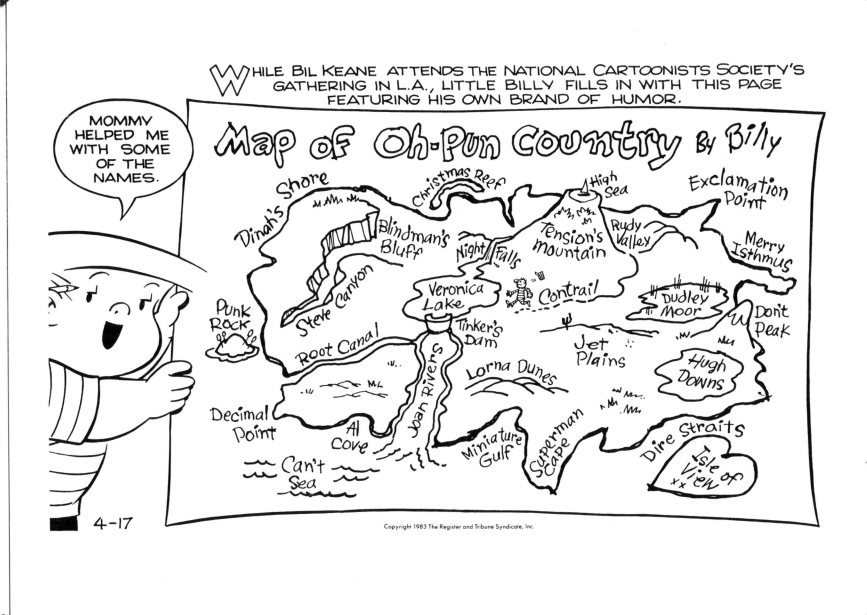

BILLY STRIKES AGAIN!

Hold on, Ruthie!

Dolly is Ruthless

Buoys and Gulls Together

Mommy Watching Her Figure

2 +2

Daddy Meating a Dead Lion

I'm being very good, Mommy!

Jeffy Lying in a Bed

PJ Kicking the Habit

Good Knight!

6-18

INTERVIEW WITH Bil Keane PART II

Q: Bil, we've covered the present status of "The Family Circus." Now tell us something about your earlier activities.

A: Well, I got up about 6:30, had a breakfast of scrambled eggs, and...

Q: I mean when you were a kid.

A: Oh. I usually had Corn Flakes, hot chocolate...

Q: As a small boy did you have a penchant for drawing?

A: No, I just used the kitchen table. In a few years when I'm older I'll probably have a penchant.

YOU AGAIN?

Q: Where were your first cartoons published?

A: In my high school magazine back in Philadelphia.

Q: Did they have the same mechanical printing capabilities back then as they have now?

A: No, Sonny. But my printer, Benjamin Franklin, was quite good.

Q: Did you take art lessons?

A: No, I taught myself to draw by imitating my favorite magazine cartoonists.

Q: Name a few of them.

A: The *New Yorker, The Saturday Evening Post, Colliers...*

Q: Wasn't the creator of "When a Feller Needs a Friend," Clare Briggs, one of your idols?

A: Absolutely. I studied everything I could about her and her personal life.

Q: Clare Briggs was a man.

A: She was? I didn't know that. "Polly and Her Pals" by Cliff Starrett was another favorite of mine because that was the name of my first girlfriend.

Q: Polly?

A: No, Cliff.

Q: I assume this also was way back in old Philadelphia?

A: Yes. I tried to date Betsy Ross but she had me flagged.

Q: Your humorous speeches are considered by many to be sharper and funnier than most stand-up comedians. What can you tell us about your personal appearances?

A: Well, I'm medium build, gray hair, glasses…

Q: Do you enjoy talking to people?

A: No, but it looks a little better than talking to myself.

Q: A good number of cartoonists are donating their original art to the Museum of Cartoon Art. Are you?

A: Our tax man advised my wife to keep the originals and donate ME to the museum.

Q: Does your wife ever provide you with fodder for your cartoons?

A: No, she provides me with the mother. I'm the fodder.

Q: Nostalgia shows through in many of your drawings.

A: It does? I'll have to use a heavier paper.

Q: What I mean is your cartoons are often colored with memories.

A: Only on Sundays. The dailies are in black and white.

Q: What direction will "The Family Circus" take in coming years?

A: I'd say in that direction over there.

Q: So will I. Goodbye Bil, and thank you for this conversation.

A: Don't mention it. To anybody.

IT'S RIGHT HERE IN BLACK AND WHITE

Daddy was without glasses up to this date. To avoid explaining to people who were always asking why I drew "myself" without glasses I added the spectacles. I'm not sure the glasses improved Daddy's eyesight that much. Otherwise, why would he wear a tie like that?

"When you said Daddy was getting glasses, I thought you meant the kind we drink out of."

"Now that Daddy's wearing glasses he doesn't look like ME any more."

"Daddy! You forgot 'em again!"

"Can you see me through your WINDOWS?"

"I forgot to tell you today's your turn to be lunch room mother at 12 o'clock!"

"I was just sittin' here taking my bath and Sam came walkin' along and FELL IN!"

"I sure hope Billy's guardian angel doesn't go on strike!"

"Mommy, we lost the sound on this key."

"If God wanted me to play the piano he'd
have given 88 fingers."

"It's not fair! You always play at the deep
end and put me in the shallow part!"

Chris doing his piano practice, 1962.

"Mommy! Dolly's losing her temperature!"

"Daddy, how old were you when Mommy let you cut
up your own meat?"

"Melanie and Buddy came over here to play 'cause
their mommy is readin' a book."

Barfy taking Jeff for a walk, 1963.

"I'll be right back, Mommy! I'm takin' Barfy for a walk!"

"I think the cake wants me to eat some of it."

"Yeah, well, you may have a better remembery than me, but I TALK gooder!"

Our daughter Gayle, whom my wife lovingly called "Dolly" when she was little, was the model for Dolly. When she was married in 1975 this cartoon appeared throughout the nation on her wedding day.

3-15

"Look, Mommy! Here comes the bride!"

5-13

"I didn't know pasghetti came in sticks."

9-27

"That's a BACK scratcher, Jeffy."

COURT JESTERS

7-21

"MOMMY! It's the ninth point of the tie-breaker and
Daddy's serving! WANNA WATCH?"

*Tennis cartoons have crept into
"The Family Circus" from time to
time because of the many hours
our entire family has spent playing
the game. In addition to umpiring
for some professional matches in
Phoenix I have gotten to play with
some fascinating people.*

STICK WITH ME, KID. I'LL GET YOU INTO THE MOVIES.

7-26

"You'll have to go someplace else to blow bubbles."

9-22
Copyright 1976
The Register and Tribune
Syndicate, Inc.

''Remember, Jeffy—if you win me you hafta
jump over the net and tell me.''

6-20
Copyright 1973
The Register and Tribune
Syndicate, Inc.

''The only thing I don't know about playin' tennis is
how to hold the bat.''

9-11
Copyright 1976
The Register and Tribune
Syndicate, Inc.

''Foot fault, double fault, play a let!
Lob it up, talk a lot, take the set!''

7-19
Copyright 1979
The Register and Tribune
Syndicate, Inc.

'''Stead of 'love' let's just say 'zero!' ''

8-24
Copyright 1973
The Register and Tribune
Syndicate, Inc.

"Mommy! My lob went over the net!"

8-30
Copyright 1974
The Register and Tribune
Syndicate, Inc.

"Oh, no! Dolly brought 'tato chips instead of the tennis balls!"

6-28
Copyright 1972
The Register and Tribune
Syndicate, Inc.

"Stop treading on PJ, Jeffy!" "I'm tellin' on YOU, Dolly!" "Quit it, Billy!"
"MOMMY!"

7-20
Copyright 1977
The Register and Tribune
Syndicate, Inc.

"After you miss a shot, you hafta look at your racket like daddy always does."

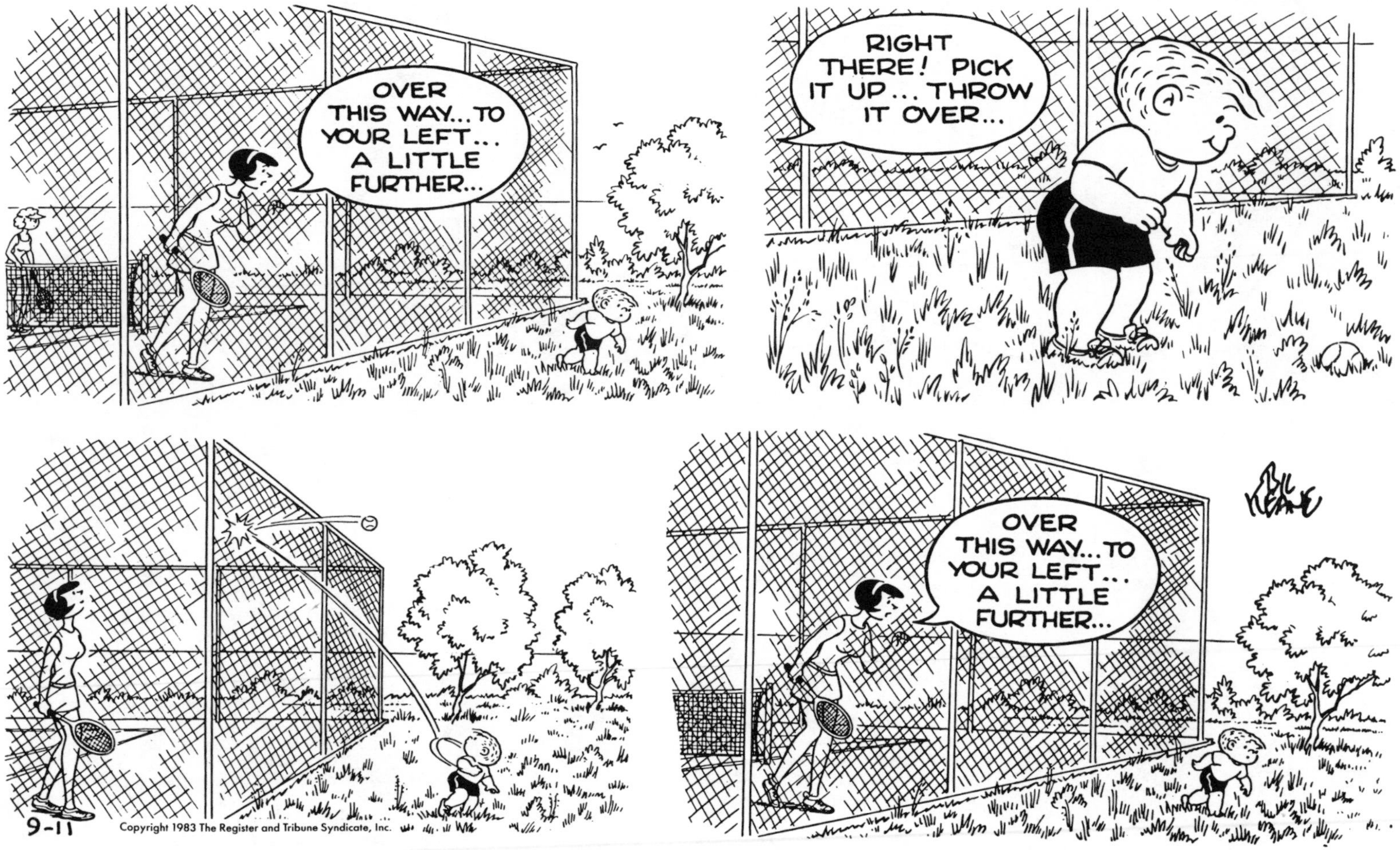
OVER THIS WAY...TO YOUR LEFT... A LITTLE FURTHER...
RIGHT THERE! PICK IT UP... THROW IT OVER...
OVER THIS WAY...TO YOUR LEFT... A LITTLE FURTHER...
9-11

Thel, Bil, Neal, Gayle, and a white frigid friend. 1953, Roslyn, PA.

WINTER NEVER LEAVES ME COLD

1-27

"Buildin' this snowman won't take long, Daddy, 'cause you have plenty of help!"

1-28

"Wow! Do you know how to build a whole snowman without readin' any 'structions, Daddy?"

1-30

"Now, can we make him a snow LADY so he won't be lonely?"

The homemade winter hat with the little pompons that Dolly usually wears was lifted from real life when Gayle was tiny. And so were the fat cheeks, button nose, etc.

1-9

"It's a snow doll!"

12-2

"When your hands and face feel very cold that's because of the chill factory."

THESE GRANDPARENTS ARE REALLY GRAND

The model for the white-haired Grandma was my own mother Florence (Bunn) Keane. My father was deceased when "The Family Circus" began, so I portrayed this Grandma as a widow.

WHY DID GRANDMA TAKE OFF HER GLASSES TO HAVE HER PICTURE TOOKEN?

3-12

Copyright 1977
The Register and Tribune
Syndicate, Inc.

"These are FUNNY, Grandma! I like lookin' at pictures of Daddy when he was little!"

3-11

Copyright 1979
The Register and Tribune
Syndicate, Inc.

"Do you use this little table and chairs very much when we're not here, Grandma?"

My dad, Al Keane, the deceased Granddad, has only been shown in family photos or as a specter of imagination. I know he would have enjoyed being a part of "The Family Circus."

"If Grandpa went to heaven just before I was borned maybe he picked me out for Mommy and Daddy."

"When Granddad went to heaven did he ever write back and tell us how he likes it?"

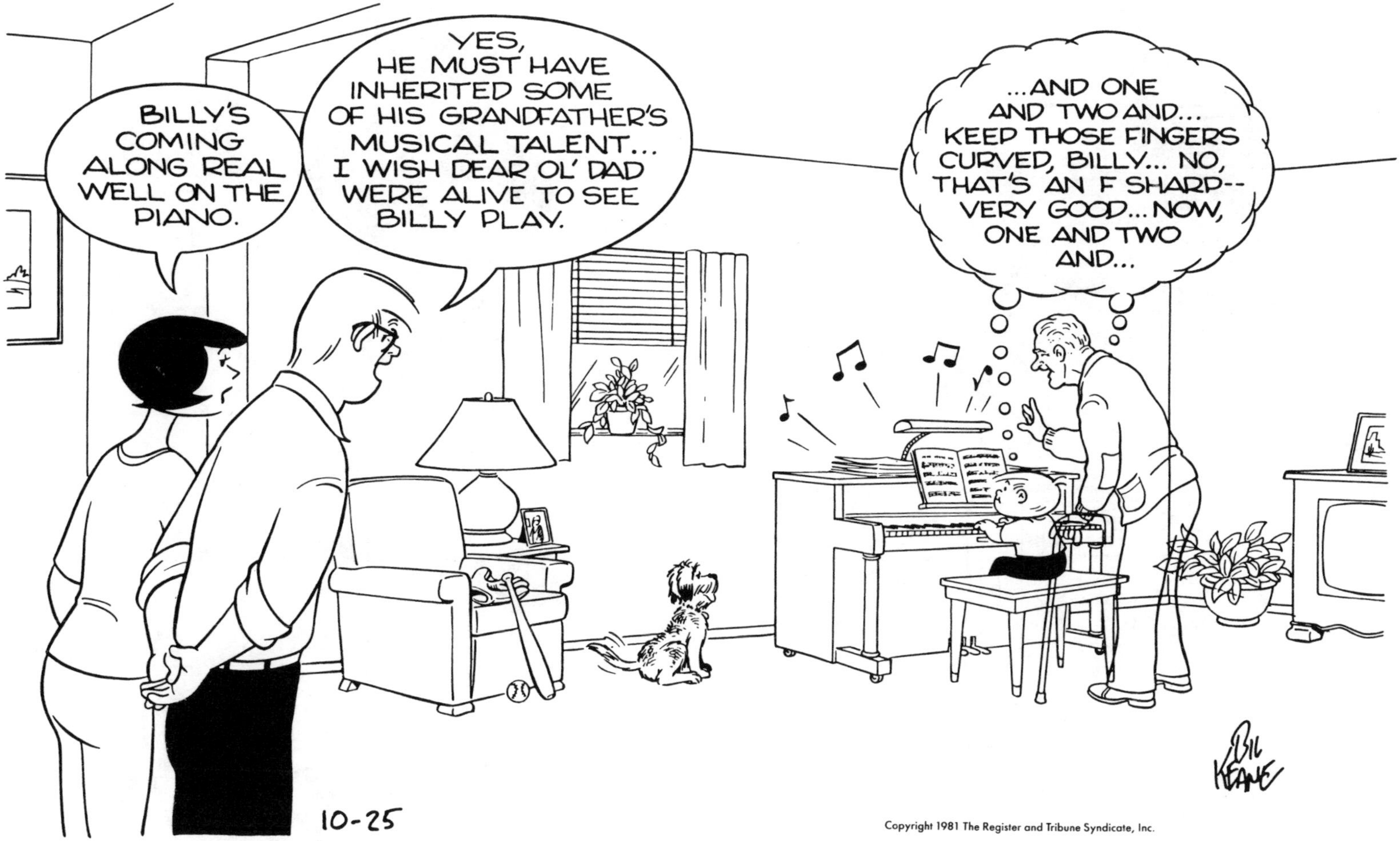
BILLY'S COMING ALONG REAL WELL ON THE PIANO.
YES, HE MUST HAVE INHERITED SOME OF HIS GRANDFATHER'S MUSICAL TALENT... I WISH DEAR OL' DAD WERE ALIVE TO SEE BILLY PLAY.
...AND ONE AND TWO AND... KEEP THOSE FINGERS CURVED, BILLY... NO, THAT'S AN F SHARP-- VERY GOOD... NOW, ONE AND TWO AND...
10-25
BIL KEANE

The other Grandma
is Esther (Mayfield)
Carne, my wife's mother.

WHY DID GRANDMA PUT ON HER GLASSES FOR THE PICTURE?

"Then what ELSE did mommy do when she was a little girl?"

"I don't think Grandma's havin' much fun here. Let's play some games with her."

"Don't worry, Grandma. Mommy says he's growin' like a weed so it'll fit him next week."

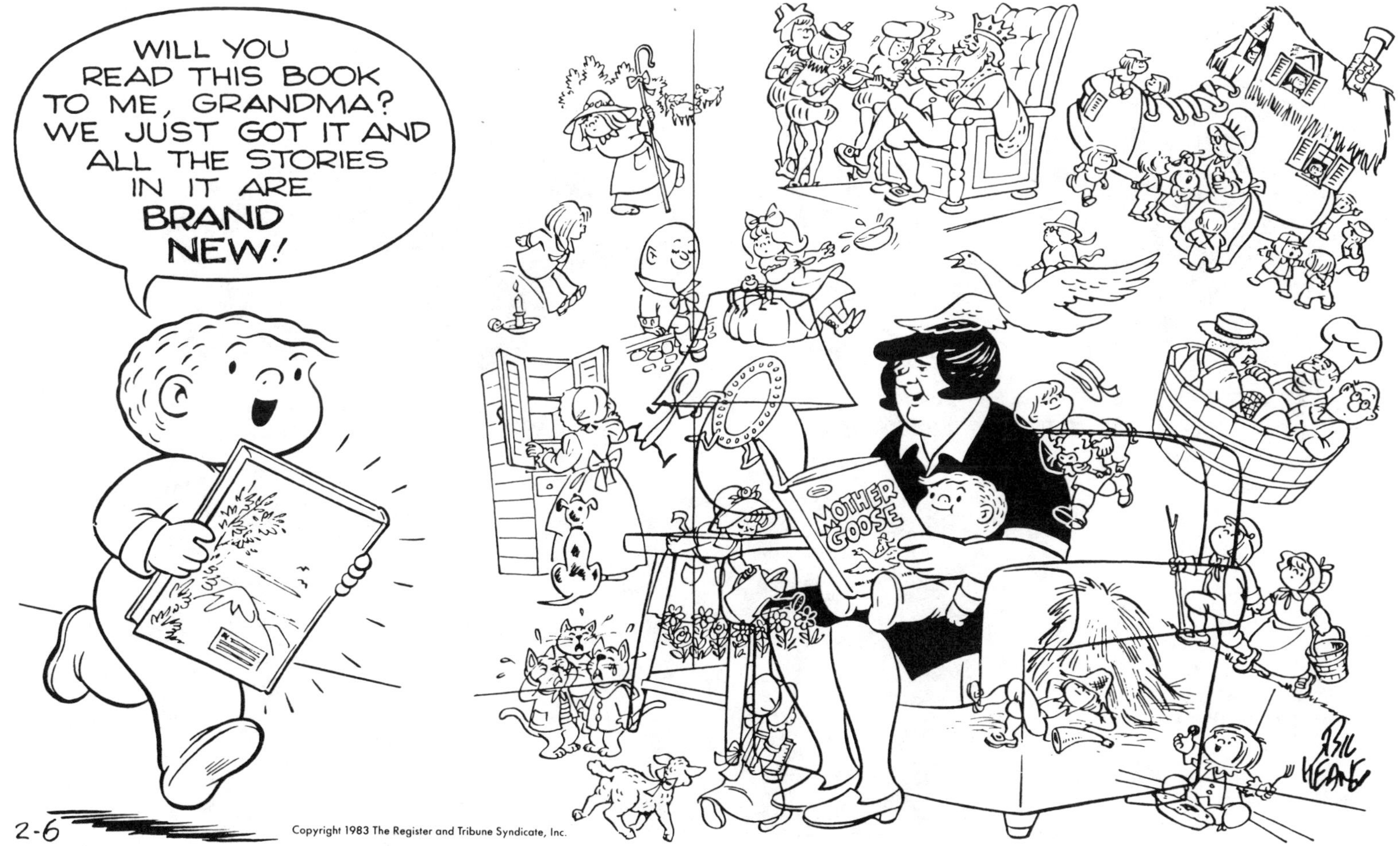
WILL YOU READ THIS BOOK TO ME, GRANDMA? WE JUST GOT IT AND ALL THE STORIES IN IT ARE BRAND NEW!
MOTHER GOOSE
2-6

12-1

"I like it when grandma and granddad are here. We can each have a grown-up."

2-8

"You could read us the comics if you want to, Granddad. But we're not allowed to ask you."

The maternal Grandma's gentle husband is Bert Carne. I have portrayed these grandparents as living in another state. In reality, their homeland is Australia.

12-3

"Daddys take you for runs and drives, but granddads take you for walks."

REMEMBER THESE?

1-12

"If you wanna see some action, go run
the can opener."

1-19

"That was very good, Dolly, but that wasn't
the Pledge of Allegiance. It was
a McDonald's commercial."

1-24

"I know you won't believe it, but this beautiful
young gal icing the cupcakes is
really my mom."

10-29

"Who finger painted the windows, Mommy?"

4-7

"Mommy, are you gonna take us to see the
Easter Bunny so we can tell him
what we want for Easter?"

4-9

"How come the Easter Bunny hides the eggs in
the same places every year?"

*Easter morning, 1961. The Easter
egg hunt.*

4-8

"Mommy, do you remember where I hid the
Easter card I made for you?"

4-17

"WOW! A RABBIT, and it's LIVE! No batteries,
no wind-up or anything! Can we keep it?"

Dear Bil,
    The selling of live creatures as toys is a barbarous practice. It often results in manhandling by children too young to know better.
    I realize you play to a family audience, but hopefully hereafter you will let your humane instincts prevail over the need for a cute gag.

                                        Sincerely,
                                        Tom E.
                                        Kansas City, MO

Dear Tom,
    Through the years we Keanes have run the gamut of pets: dogs, cats, rabbits, birds, ducks, turtles, fish, snakes—you name it. Our kids learned a little something about life, responsibility, and even death from each pet.
    I don't advocate cruelty to animals in any way, and appreciate your views. But small children and animals are a good combination.

                                        Best regards,
                                        Bil Keane

*Glen (right) shares Snowball, our
pet rabbit, with a friend. 1967.*

4-29

"Speak! Come on, Snowball, speak!"

This was the night the nation got to see us on TV for the first time: Feb. 10, 1978, when our Valentine Special aired on NBC. It was subsequently followed by a Christmas Special and one for Easter.

"Oh, boy! Tonight we get to see ourselves on TV! Turn on the set, Daddy, it's time for the special!"

"How will that stuff get from down there up to my sore throat?"

"I'm gonna say my prayers, Daddy. Is there anything you want?"

FOOLING MOTHER NATURE

Mother Nature and the Four Seasons are
favorite topics for whimsical "Family
Circus" cartoons throughout the year.

"Why do trees take their clothes off when it
starts getting cold?"

"Wind is air in a hurry."

1-26

"Spring doesn't come till they run out of snow."

Each winter I like to include some snow scenes. Living in the Arizona desert we don't see snow as a large portion of the country does, but my memories of earlier years in Pennsylvania provide me with inspiration (without the frostbite).

BUT WE NEVER GET TO GO SLEDDIN'!

1-14

"God put topping on everything!"

2-19

"How do you KNOW each snowflake is different? They all look alike to me."

"Look! These dandelions have turned into little pompons!"

"If March comes in like a lion it goes out like a light. Right, Mommy?"

"When clouds get mad they rain on you."

"They flash the lightning to warn you that the thunder is coming."

"The sun is going down into its nest to sleep."

"If trees were people, they'd get a ticket for littering."

"Smile, Grandma! God's taking our picture!"

"Don't be afraid. The lightning won't strike
you as long as Mommy's out here."

5-1

THE GREMLINS

A popular addition to the "Circus" occasionally is that invisible gremlin "Not Me." Judging from the mail, this little character lives in everybody's house. And so does his girlfriend "Ida Know."

"Who ate up my whole box of candy?"

"Not me!"
"Not me!"
"Not me!"

"Who splashed that water on the floor?"

"Not me!"
"Not me!"

"Who took the pencil that belongs here?"

"Not me!"
"Not me!"

"Who had my pinking shears?"
"Ida Know."

"Who crossed out 'broccoli' on my grocery list?"
"Ida know."   "Ida know."   "Ida know."

"Who got out all
these toys?"   "Ida Know."

"Okay, who threw the frisbee?"
"Ida Know."
"Not me."

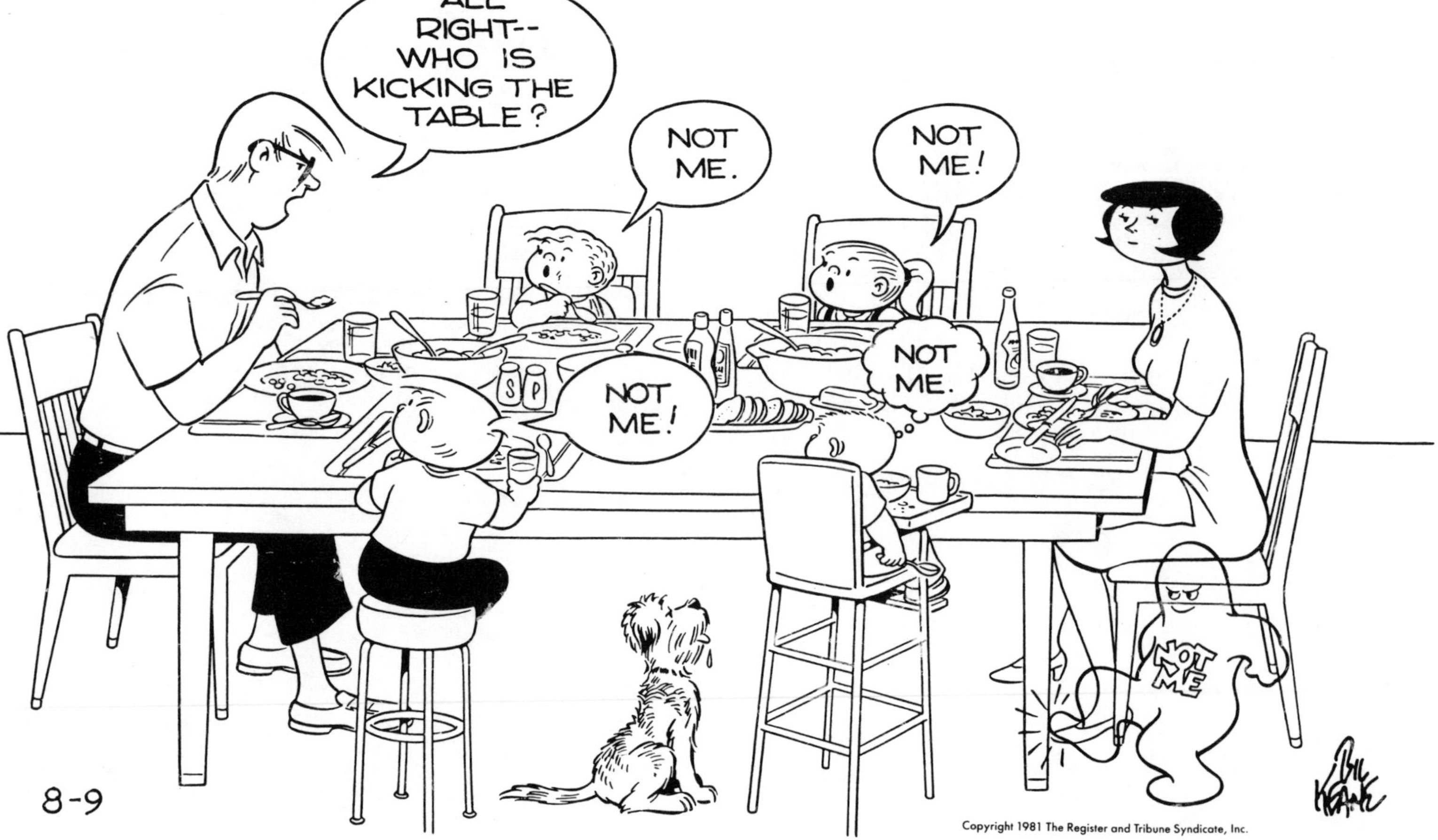
ALL RIGHT-- WHO IS KICKING THE TABLE?
NOT ME.
NOT ME!
NOT ME!
NOT ME.
NOT ME
8-9
BIL KEANE

GETTING THE SHOW ON THE ROAD

Summer Vacations are major happenings in most families and each year "The Family Circus" gets away from it all (at times it seems we take it all *with* us) to a different location.

Fans look forward to the annual treks which usually last for several weeks. All the vacation situations are based on trips we have taken in the past with the children.

Get out your road map, motel guide, and credit card. On these next dozen or so pages are a sampling of our vacation escapades.

7-19

Copyright 1973
The Register and Tribune
Syndicate, Inc.

"Calm down! CALM DOWN! We don't leave on vacation till SATURDAY!"

"Mommy, can Kathy go on vacation with us? She wouldn't take up much room."

"I woke PJ up so he can help us watch for deer!"

"Gulls are lucky. They stay at the seashore all year."

Gayle and Glen, 1957.

This three-year-old inspiration cavorting in the ocean in 1957 is our middle child Glen, who has put all that animation and action to good use. He is now a successful animator for Walt Disney Productions.

7-3

Copyright 1976
The Register and Tribune
Syndicate, Inc.

"Billy, you better stay in the shallow end."

8-6

Copyright 1976
The Register and Tribune
Syndicate, Inc.

"MOMMY!"

Neal, Thel, and Gayle, 1955.

8-19

"Wow! There's sure a lot of sand down here!"

7-23

"You'll never empty out the whole ocean yourself,
PJ! Here—I'll help you!"

7-28

"NO! NO!"

7-29
Copyright 1976
The Register and Tribune
Syndicate, Inc.

"Can't we wait t'see if it stops, Mommy?
Maybe it's just a SHOWER!"

Bil:
    My wife and family love your cartoons. I love your wife. Does Thel look as good in real life as in the comic?

                    Bert T.
                    Dunedin, FL.

Bert: Better!   Bil

8-30
Copyright 1980
The Register and Tribune
Syndicate, Inc.

"Will you put this in your pocket, Mommy?"

"Daddy doesn't need a life jacket 'cause the
captain has to go down with the ship."

"Why are you going so slow, Daddy? We'll NEVER
get there."

HISTORICAL
MARKER
AHEAD

"Aw! Do we hafta stop and get out again, Daddy?"

"Where does he keep the pork chops?"

"I hope the pilot tells us when we get to New York so we don't go past our stop."

"Why does that man keep talkin' to us, Daddy? Does he KNOW us?"

"That's the Canadian flag and the next one is —No, that's Australian, then next in Spain—No, wait...Sweden! Then, I think that's either Italy or Ireland and..."

The family at the U.N., 1967.

8-12

"Don't keep lookin' up at the buildings!
People will know we're from outta town!"

8-19

"Mommy, will you hold my dollar just
in case I get mugged?"

8-29

"Aren't we gonna get goin' any faster than
this?"

9-3

"We HAFTA go home, Jeffy! Daddy ran out
of money."

8-30
Copyright 1971
The Register and Tribune
Syndicate, Inc.

"I had a nice time, my lunch was delicious and tell the pilot that was a very good landing."

8-31
Copyright 1971
The Register and Tribune
Syndicate, Inc.

"I'll find it, Daddy! It's the one with PJ's teddy bear on the back seat."

Bil and the boys, Redwood Forest, California, 1966.

7-4
Copyright 1983
The Register and Tribune
Syndicate, Inc.

"Boy! You'd need a lot of rope to hang a swing from that!"

"For the last time shut that darn thing off and let's go sightseeing!"

"Was Abraham Lincoln really that big?"

"This is my favorite historical site, Daddy, 'cause we get to ride the elevator."

"NOW I 'member where my bathing suit is! Is it very far back to the railing outside the motel we stayed at last night?"

8-26

"I'm movin' to the non-smoking section."

Camping, White Mountains,
Arizona, 1962.

8-25

"Where can I buy a post card? Grandma said to
be sure to send her one."

8-11

"It's only an owl. Now, get back in your
own sleeping bag!"

Our cabin, Wyoming, 1967.

"Aren't we going to the BEACH this year?"

"Time for vacation to begin, Daddy."

Bil and Gayle, 1952.

Jeff and Thel, South Rim of the Grand Canyon.

"Wish they had something like this between our house and the school!"

"This is like a church, Mommy. Everyone's whispering."

"I saw it on TV once, but it looked littler."

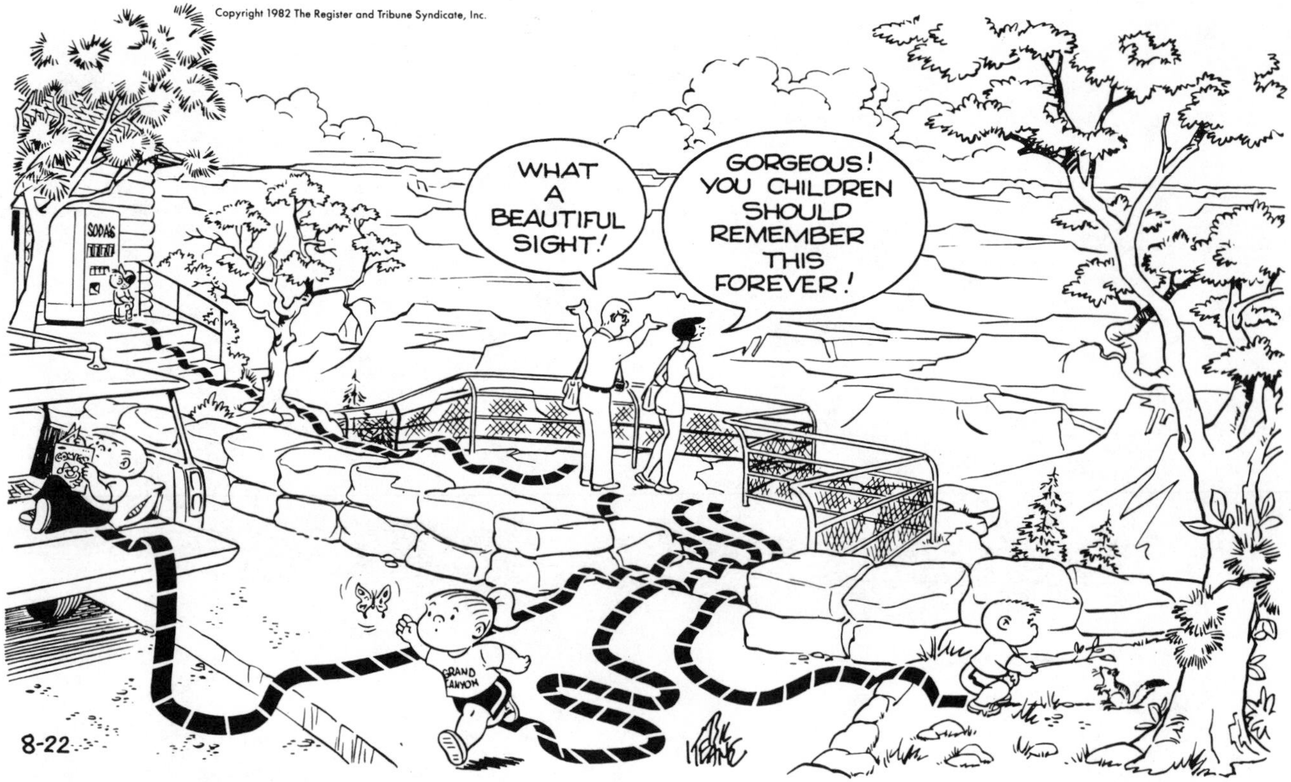
Copyright 1982 The Register and Tribune Syndicate, Inc.
SODA'S
WHAT A BEAUTIFUL SIGHT!
GORGEOUS! YOU CHILDREN SHOULD REMEMBER THIS FOREVER!
GRAND CANYON
8-22

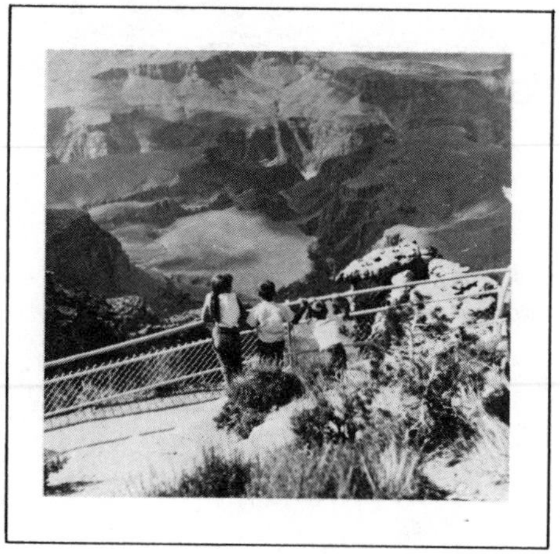

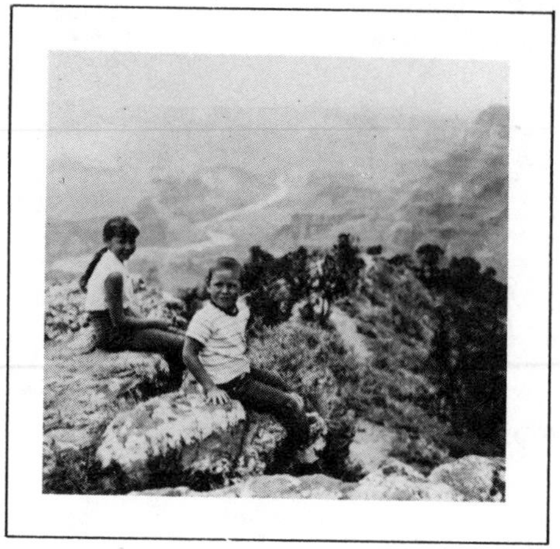

At the Grand Canyon, 1960.

MORE COLOR RECEPTION

A Roadside Stop, Utah.

Surveying the bear damage to our ice chest, Yellowstone Park, 1964.

Glen, Neal, and Gayle at Disneyland in 1960 when they were more the size of Mickey Mouse.

Probably the most popular of the formats I use for the
Sunday pages is the "dotted-line" showing the circuitous
route Billy, or at times one of the other members of the
family, takes in getting from one place to another. It is
almost like a game or puzzle for a reader to follow the path
in and out, over, under, and around to the final destina-
tion. These scenes take longer than usual to draw, but
they're fun to do as long as I don't run out of patience.

Dear Bil Keane,
"The Family Circus" has always been a pleasurable part of my perusal of the Sunday paper. Your understanding of the psyche of children is wonderful. You obviously love children. How then, sir, could you possibly have drawn the picture enclosed? I cannot believe that you would draw a Clorox bottle (extreme right in the middle) as a part of the mess.
I know that comics are make-believe, but they also set an example. You can have humor without danger.
An observant fan
(Mrs.) Elizabeth P.
New Hartford, NY

Dear Elizabeth,
That's a half-gallon plastic milk bottle. Thanks for your concern.
Love from
"The Family Circus,"
Bil Keane

Incidentally, what dolly is viewing on the TV screen is "Dim Viewer" talking with "Aunt Tenna," two characters from a syndicated cartoon "Channel Chuckles" which I drew from 1954 to 1976 when my picture tube burned out.

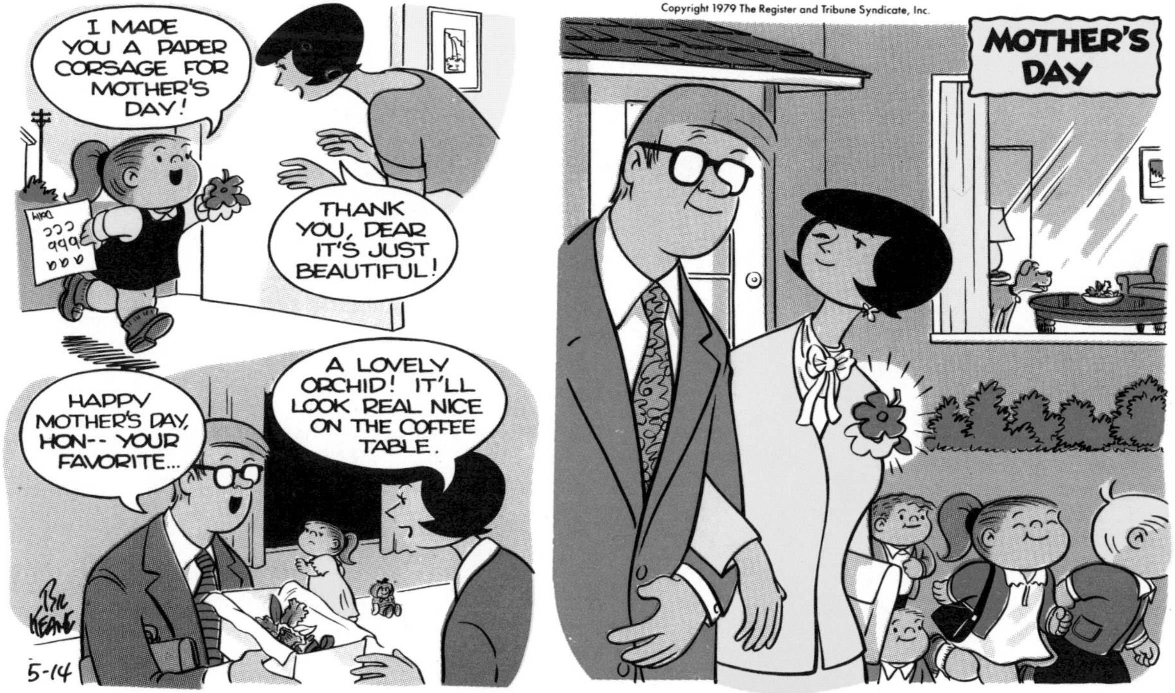
I MADE YOU A PAPER CORSAGE FOR MOTHER'S DAY!
THANK YOU, DEAR IT'S JUST BEAUTIFUL!
HAPPY MOTHER'S DAY, HON-- YOUR FAVORITE...
A LOVELY ORCHID! IT'LL LOOK REAL NICE ON THE COFFEE TABLE.
5-14
MOTHER'S DAY

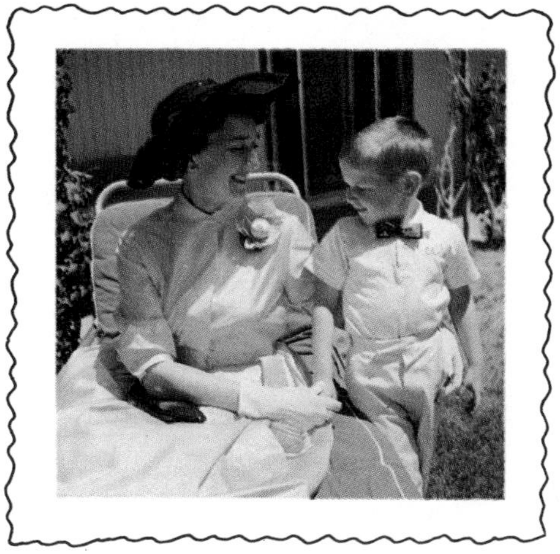

Thel with corsage made for her in kindergarten by Chris, 1960 (she wore it to church).

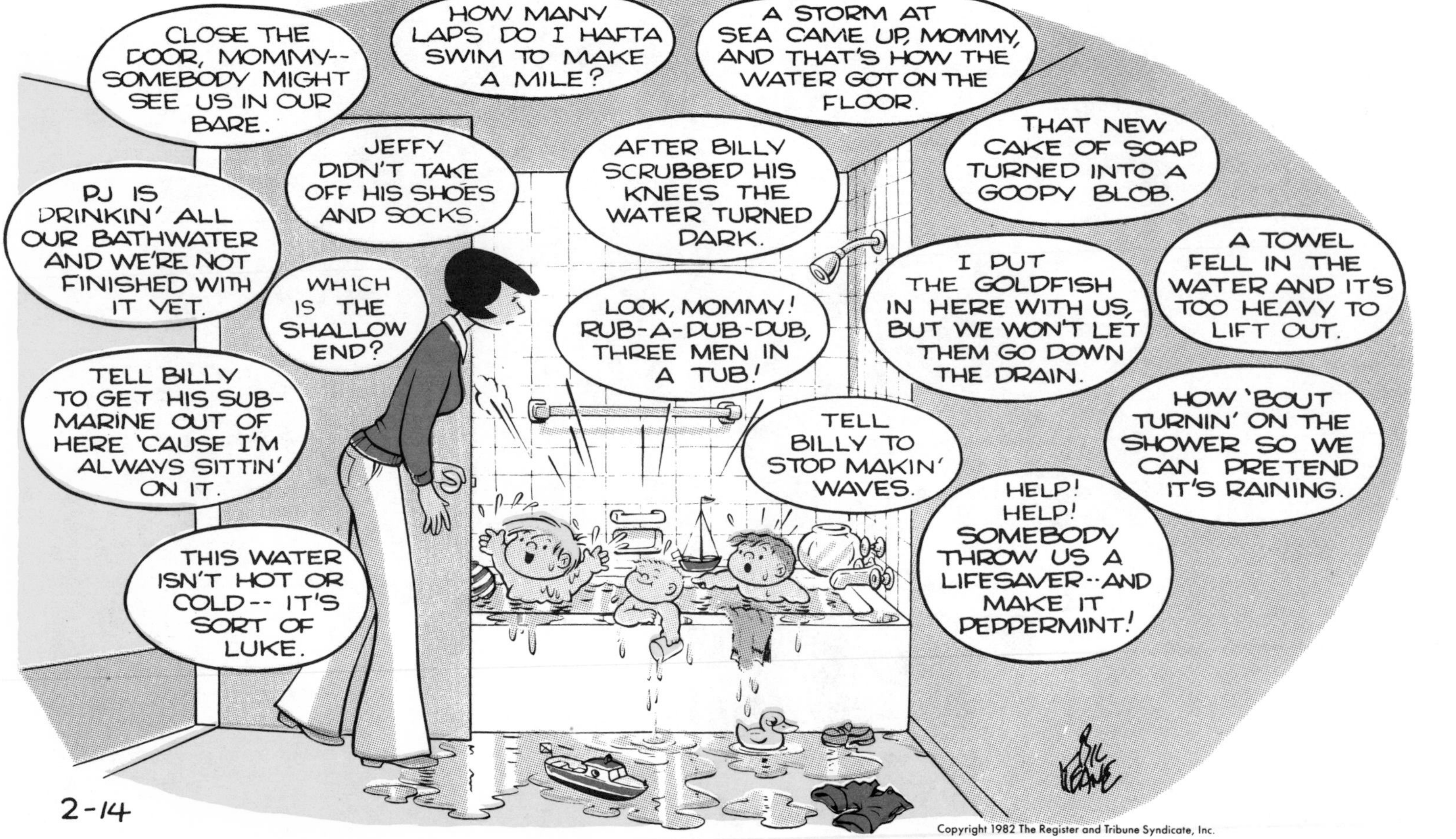
CLOSE THE DOOR, MOMMY-- SOMEBODY MIGHT SEE US IN OUR BARE.
HOW MANY LAPS DO I HAFTA SWIM TO MAKE A MILE?
A STORM AT SEA CAME UP, MOMMY, AND THAT'S HOW THE WATER GOT ON THE FLOOR.
JEFFY DIDN'T TAKE OFF HIS SHOES AND SOCKS.
AFTER BILLY SCRUBBED HIS KNEES THE WATER TURNED DARK.
THAT NEW CAKE OF SOAP TURNED INTO A GOOPY BLOB.
PJ IS DRINKIN' ALL OUR BATHWATER AND WE'RE NOT FINISHED WITH IT YET.
WHICH IS THE SHALLOW END?
LOOK, MOMMY! RUB-A-DUB-DUB, THREE MEN IN A TUB!
I PUT THE GOLDFISH IN HERE WITH US, BUT WE WON'T LET THEM GO DOWN THE DRAIN.
A TOWEL FELL IN THE WATER AND IT'S TOO HEAVY TO LIFT OUT.
TELL BILLY TO GET HIS SUB-MARINE OUT OF HERE 'CAUSE I'M ALWAYS SITTIN' ON IT.
TELL BILLY TO STOP MAKIN' WAVES.
HOW 'BOUT TURNIN' ON THE SHOWER SO WE CAN PRETEND IT'S RAINING.
HELP! HELP! SOMEBODY THROW US A LIFESAVER--AND MAKE IT PEPPERMINT!
THIS WATER ISN'T HOT OR COLD-- IT'S SORT OF LUKE.
2-14

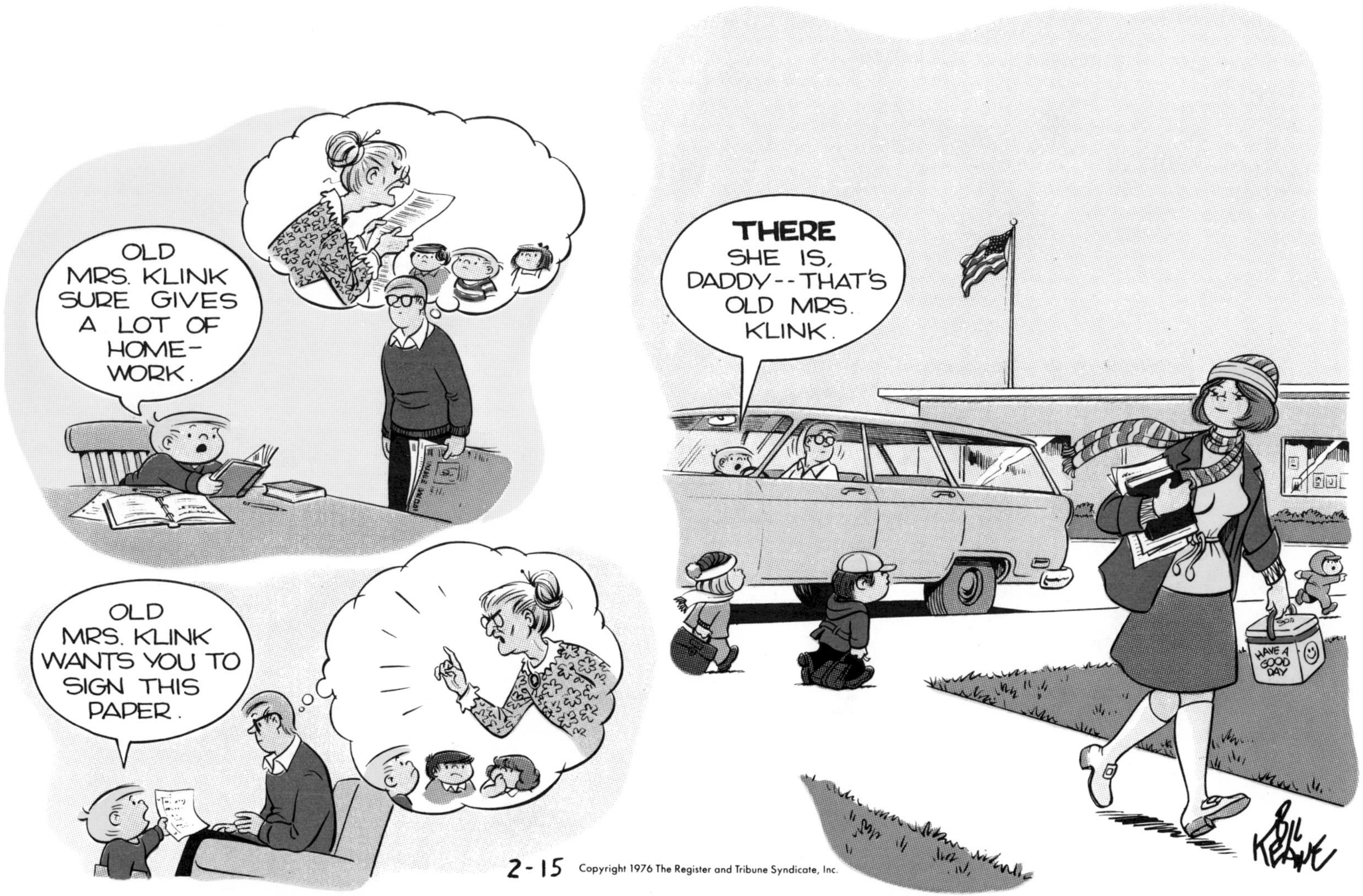
OLD MRS. KLINK SURE GIVES A LOT OF HOME-WORK.
OLD MRS. KLINK WANTS YOU TO SIGN THIS PAPER.
THERE SHE IS, DADDY--THAT'S OLD MRS. KLINK.
HAVE A GOOD DAY

2-15

Of course Billy, Dolly, Jeffy, and PJ will
never age beyond their present 7, 5, 3, and
18 months. But once in a while in a phan-
tasy or thought balloon I will show how
things might be in the future. This cartoon
traces Billy's life from cradle to present,
then into the future till he breezes out the
front door forever.

Chris, 1958.

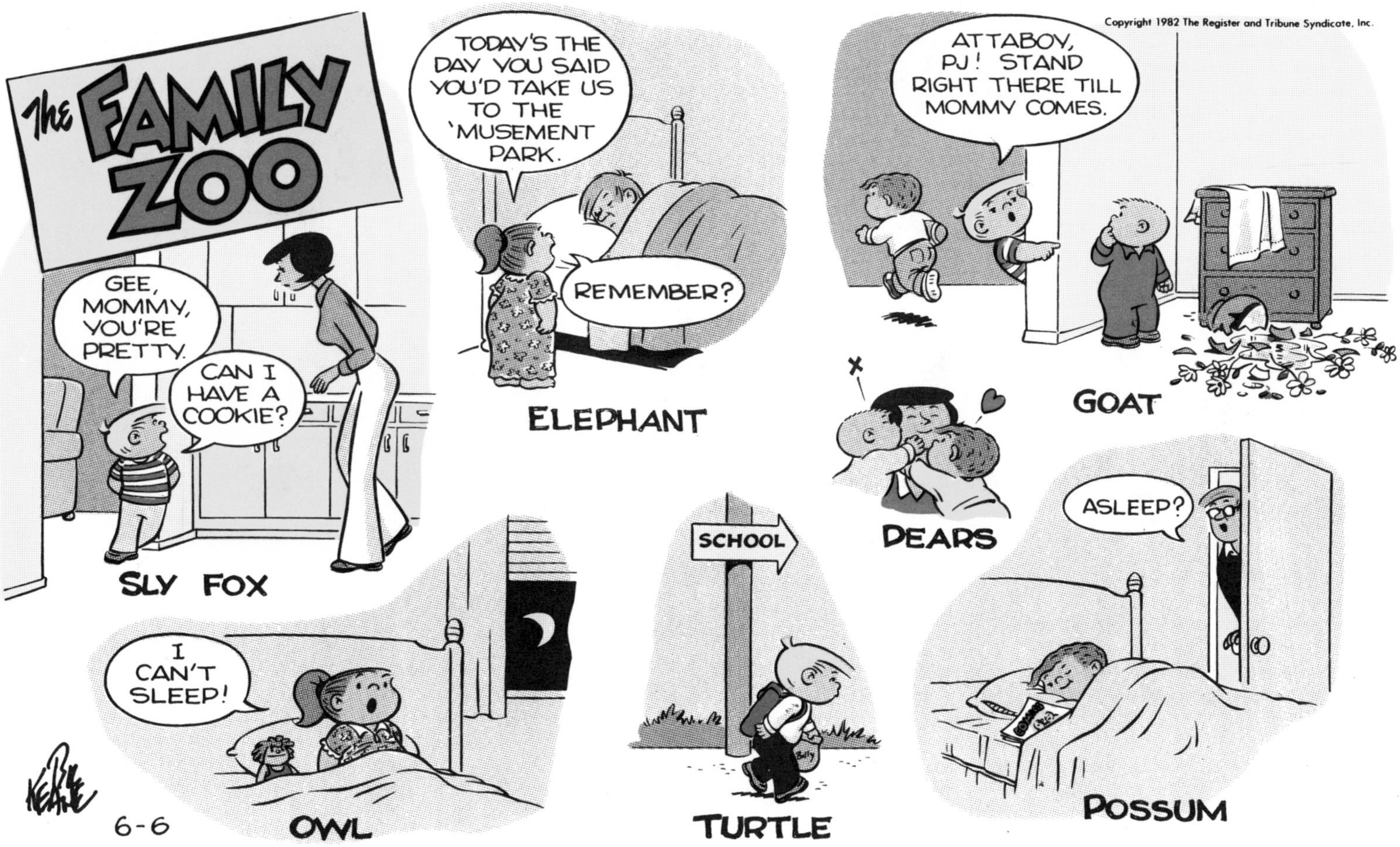

The FAMILY ZOO
GEE, MOMMY, YOU'RE PRETTY.
CAN I HAVE A COOKIE?
SLY FOX
TODAY'S THE DAY YOU SAID YOU'D TAKE US TO THE 'MUSEMENT PARK.
REMEMBER?
ELEPHANT
Copyright 1982 The Register and Tribune Syndicate, Inc.
ATTABOY, PJ! STAND RIGHT THERE TILL MOMMY COMES.
GOAT
DEARS
I CAN'T SLEEP!
OWL
SCHOOL
TURTLE
ASLEEP?
POSSUM
6-6

Dear Bil,
    Simply cannot resist a word about yester-day's strip, "Is this the little girl I carried", etc. Egad how that hit me.
    I am 72 and my lovable lady brats are now 39 and 40. I frequently look back and mope over what I shooda done.
    Musta been "too busy" at the wrong times just like Daddio in your strip.
    Thanx for a lovely sentimental touch.
                                    Dave B.
                                    West Orange, NJ

Dear Bil Keane:
    Your Sunday strip yesterday "Sunrise, Sunset" from "Fiddler on the Roof" touched a nerve.
    For years, even a snatch of the tune has triggered the floodgates.
    For years, also, your work has caught the essence of childhood, growing older, the transience of life, the eternal verities.
    The combination yesterday was devastating.
    Many thanks,
                                    Bob S.
                                    Hardened Executive
                                    Phila. PA

Sir:
    Please re-run your 1-25 ('80 or '81) strip and let us find Grandmother's other shoe. I put this strip on my bedroom wall where everyone (young and old) could play "Hunt the Shoe." We have about worn the paper out, and can find only one shoe. I have 8 grandchildren and several neighbor children that love to have their turn looking.
                                    Sincerely,
                                    (Mrs.) Leon E.
                                    Glen, MS

Dear Mrs. E.
    Just for you, here is the other shoe.

Dear Mr. Keane,
    I am 9½ and I am writing to let you know my mother read your Sunday comic last night and woke me up to say she loves me. I didn't mind at all. Thank you.
                                                Jason W.
                                                Columbus, OH

Dear Bil,

I am writing in response to your drawing of this morning, the one of the old house. That is one of the most moving drawings you, or anyone else, had made. It brought tears to my eyes. As one grows older, the passage of time becomes more precious. Your cartoon makes me understand more about my time here.

All Best,

Terry G.
Claremont, CA

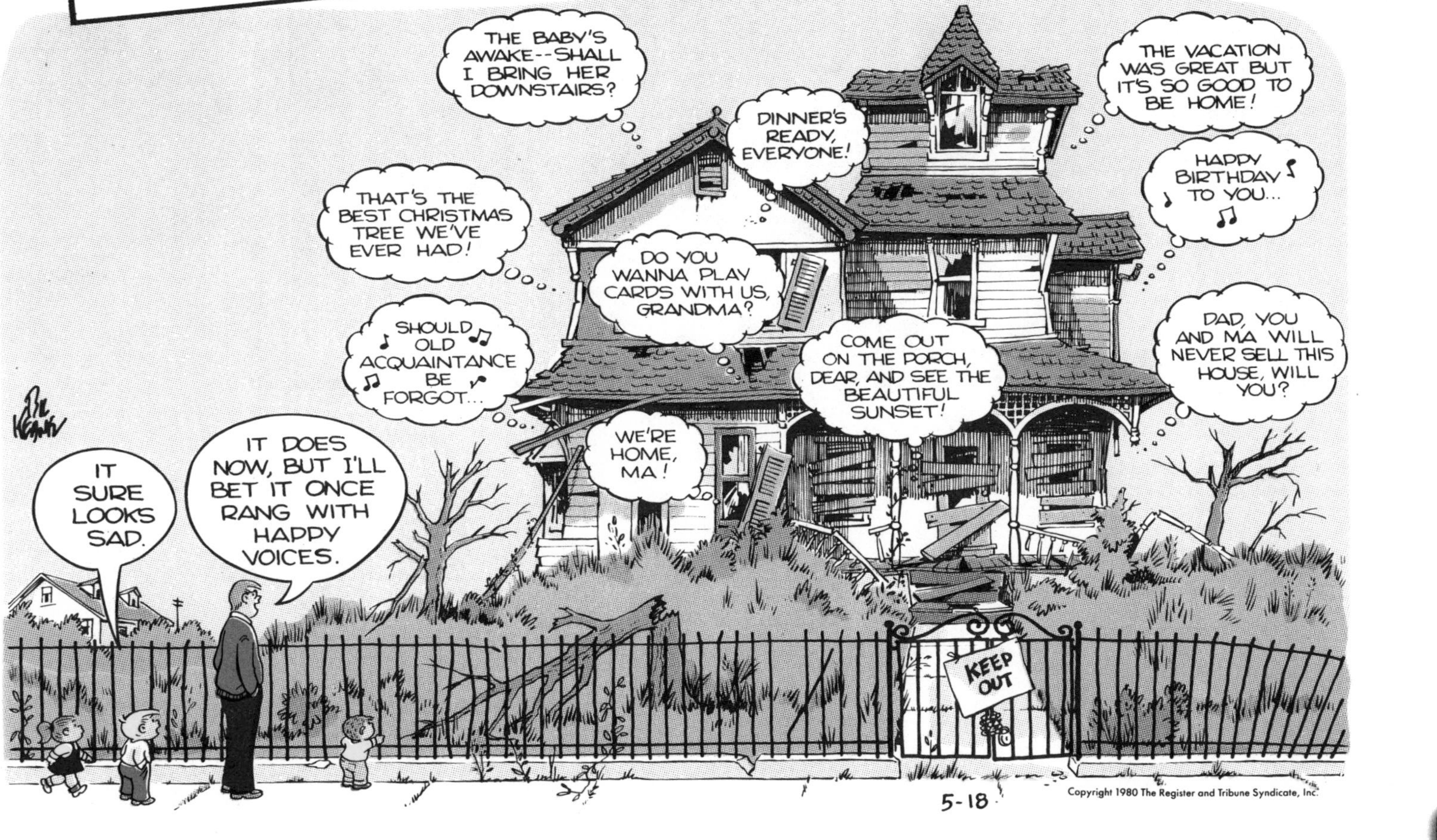
IT SURE LOOKS SAD.
IT DOES NOW, BUT I'LL BET IT ONCE RANG WITH HAPPY VOICES.
THAT'S THE BEST CHRISTMAS TREE WE'VE EVER HAD!
SHOULD OLD ACQUAINTANCE BE FORGOT...
THE BABY'S AWAKE--SHALL I BRING HER DOWNSTAIRS?
DO YOU WANNA PLAY CARDS WITH US, GRANDMA?
WE'RE HOME, MA!
DINNER'S READY, EVERYONE!
COME OUT ON THE PORCH, DEAR, AND SEE THE BEAUTIFUL SUNSET!
THE VACATION WAS GREAT BUT IT'S SO GOOD TO BE HOME!
HAPPY BIRTHDAY TO YOU...
DAD, YOU AND MA WILL NEVER SELL THIS HOUSE, WILL YOU?
KEEP OUT
5-18

Dear Bil,
We love your cartoon and especially the dotted track ones. However, as a professional architect, I must criticize your drawing of the house. It just won't work.
Robert M. B.
Wilmington, DE

Dear Mr. B.,
I have seen some cartoons drawn by architects and they didn't work either.
Best wishes,
Bil Keane

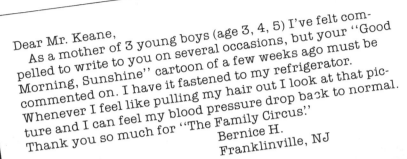

Dear Mr. Keane,
 As a mother of 3 young boys (age 3, 4, 5) I've felt compelled to write to you on several occasions, but your "Good Morning, Sunshine" cartoon of a few weeks ago must be commented on. I have it fastened to my refrigerator. Whenever I feel like pulling my hair out I look at that picture and I can feel my blood pressure drop back to normal. Thank you so much for "The Family Circus."
                                        Bernice H.
                                        Franklinville, NJ

10-14

Dear Mr. Keane,
Have the "Home and Families of America" made you an honorary member yet? They're missing the boat if they haven't.
Your 11-9 cartoon encompassed the sounds, aromas, voices, faces, etc. that add up to "love," the most important ingredient in any home. A brilliant cartoon.

Sincerely,
Lucille LaG.
Pittsburgh, PA

Dear Bil,
Often I've wanted to write a fan letter to you. And now I'm doing it.
The bright, warm, welcoming home you depicted today says it all. And I just loved the cat lying on the chair purring. That's contentment.
Keep us laughing, thinking, remembering, and loving.

Mrs. Margery B.
Boston, MA

PLEASE STAND BY

TV has become a major influence in most American homes. "The Family Circus" reflects the impact on children's lives.

THEN WHY DO WE ALWAYS HAFTA GO TO BED WHEN IT'S PRIME TIME?

3-11

"We'll be right there as soon as we see the end of this commercial!"

12-1

"Mommy, the picture's a little woozy."

5-19

Copyright 1978
The Register and Tribune
Syndicate, Inc.

"He's a real good actor. He makes you think
he LIKES kissing girls."

Jeff and Chris glued to the tube.

MR. CHAIRMAN,
MR. CHAIRMAN...

7-14

Copyright 1976
The Register and Tribune
Syndicate, Inc.

Boy! The TV programs on vacation aren't as
good as the ones we watch at home."

2-28

Copyright 1977
The Register and Tribune
Syndicate, Inc.

"I think heaven is on television."

2-11

"Is he going to do the dishes?"

1-13

"I like this kind of guitar music—one
thread at a time."

February 28, 1983

Dear Bil:
   You would not believe the avalanche
of mail I have received as a result of
your cartoon.
   I've had cartoons sent to me on
white paper, green paper, orange
paper. They have ranged from about
2" x 2" to about 3" x 5."
   It's incredible!!! And the cartoon
itself was so delightful...what more
can I say.
      Again, many thanks,
                  Willard Scott
                  Today Show,
                  NBC

2-15

"Willard Scott's forecasts aren't always
100 percent accurate."

"I don't think this is recommended for mature
audiences."

"It's the Morman Tavernapple Choir."

"Do they only have one channel?"

"But, Grandma! We don't watch 'As the
World Turns'. This is when we always
watch 'Sesame Street!'"

4-5

"I bet her kids hear her when she calls them."

Gayle, Glen, and Neal mesmerized by Lassie, 1958.

10-20

"Shall I give it a whack like mommy always does?"

10-2

"Their mommies are gonna be mad. They're playin' in the mud."

"Practice faster, Billy. We can't turn on TV till you're finished!"

"I'd rather watch TV with you, Grandma. All Daddy watches is football games."

"Daddy, will you hitch up the video games for me?"

"Come quick, Mommy. The picture's wrinkled!"

2-27

Copyright 1977 The Register and Tribune Syndicate, Inc.

The cartoon character Billy is watching on TV is "Silly Philly," a weekly comic page I drew for the Philadelphia Bulletin where I worked as staff artist from 1945 to 1959.

THE BEST OF CIRCLES

"All right, let's try the song again—and, Billy, you be a listener."

"Daddy, you sing bass and we'll sing trouble."

"Miss Lee is gettin' married and we have to learn to spell her new name. It's Mihaleckovich!"

Dear Mr. Keane,
I've been reading and laughing at your cartoons for some time now, but tonight's didn't strike me as funny.
I hate to think how poor Billy felt in response to his teacher's comment. Will he ever sing again? How long will he be ridiculed by his classmates because of his teacher's short-sighted criticism?
I'm sure you didn't realize the seriousness of your cartoon as I've come to know you are a humane person through your sensitive work.

Sincerely,
Terri R.
Brookline, MA

Dear Terri,
I was just telling it like it is (or was). Yes, he WILL sing again. In spite of his teacher. I know. I was the kid told to be a listener.
Both Billy and I appreciate your comments.

Best wishes,
Bil Keane

11-22
Copyright 1982
The Register and Tribune
Syndicate, Inc.

"Miss Johnson was absent today. We had a
pretend teacher."

Dear Mr. Keane,
    In reference to your cartoon of
Nov. 22, 1982—How dare you refer
to a substitute teacher as a pretend
teacher! Shame on you! We are very
capable teachers who can take over
for another teacher at the last
minute. Please refer to us as *Pro* not
pretend.

                    Sincerely,
                    Marilyn T.
                    Lancaster, NY

Dear Marilyn,
    "Substitute teachers are pros, not
pretend"...I'll write it 50 times.
Sorry. Much love to you all.
                    Bil Keane
                    Pretend Cartoonist

Talk about a loose shoestring operation!
Billy's right shoestring has been untied in
many cartoons for the past decade. Not his
left but only his *RIGHT* shoestring. And
only Billy. Why? No reason. Just a little-
noticed detail that might add to the
"typical" aspect of "The Family Circus."
However, with the appearance of Velcro on
kids' shoes, I'll probably eliminate the loose
shoestring to keep the feature up-to-date.

10-3
Copyright 1977
The Register and Tribune
Syndicate, Inc.

"I'm never wearin' this shirt to school again! I
got called on five times today!"

"The painter's here and he brought us passes
for today at the zoo!"

"I'll never understand girls if I live to be 13."

The "Falcons" pennant which I draw on
the wall of Billy's room is enjoyed by many
football fans in Georgia who have written to
thank me for plugging the Atlanta Falcons.
However, "Falcons" was the name of the
football team at Northeast Catholic High
School in Philadelphia where my first
cartoons were published in the school
magazine.

"Not bad, but I'd advise you not to plan on a
career in the military."

6-26

"Okay! Let's watch the movie!"

5-3

"Wow! Is that man gonna have a baby?"

11-18

"Mommy! The toilet won't stop tinkling."

Still rated "G" the newspaper comics are more lenient today than 25 years ago. In 1960 I would not have had Dolly saying "toilet" or "tinkling," and would *NEVER* have drawn the John, for heaven's sake!

"We ARE in bed!"

"Enjoy them every minute, Deary. Before you can turn around they'll be grown."

The boys climbing Camelback Mountain, 1966.

"Why do they hafta put all the good views on top of hills?"

"Look at it this way—Erma Bombeck would probably find something very amusing about this."

Occasionally I will use the name of a friend or neighbor. Erma Bombeck is both. I collaborated with her on a book "Just Wait Till You Have Children of Your Own" in 1971.

MOMMY SAYS ERMA BOMBECK MUST BE LOOKIN' IN **OUR** WINDOW!

"He's cryin' because the wolf scared him."

"I'll wash, you dry."

"I'm practicing to be a daddy."

Chris getting a piggyback ride from Glen, 1960.

"Daddy, I like it when Mommy's playin' tennis and you cook the dinner."

"You can tell saints 'cause they always wear ring hats."

6-28

"Keep watching, and maybe we'll get
to see his head go indoors."

Glen inspects pet turtle with Gayle,
1955.

Brother reading to brother, 1962.

9-11

"Little Miss Muffet sat on a tuppet eating her spiders
away..."

6-4

Copyright 1979
The Register and Tribune
Syndicate, Inc.

"Billy! You better hold Daddy's hand so that if
an animal escapes it won't eat you!"

6-14

Copyright 1979
The Register and Tribune
Syndicate, Inc.

"Come back, Dolly. He's not through
looking at you."

6-7

Copyright 1979
The Register and Tribune
Syndicate, Inc.

"They remember even longer than mommies."

5-1

Copyright 1975
The Register and Tribune
Syndicate, Inc.

"Wow! Look! ANTS!"

8-30

Copyright 1982
The Register and Tribune
Syndicate, Inc.

"And I wasn't even allowed to keep a FROG in my room!"

9-7

Copyright 1982
The Register and Tribune
Syndicate, Inc.

"I heard a strange noise out in the garage."

Dear Mr. Keane,
I have been a reader/collector of comics for years. Your cartoons of Aug. 30 and Sept. 7 about E.T. excel in artwork, humor, and quality. Is there any way that I can purchase the originals?

Nancy S. B.
San Mateo, CA

Dear Nancy,
Sorry, the originals have already been sold to another California reader. Guy named Steven Spielberg.
Best wishes,
Bil Keane

"Will sucking on that piece of glass help make Billy better?"

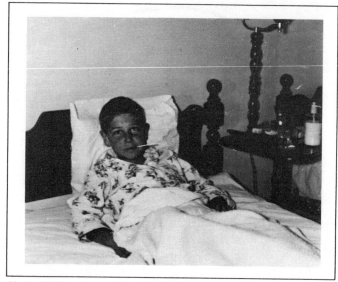

Chris, 1967.

"Feel my head and see if I have a headache!"

"You'll hear a lot more goin' on if you'll put that thing on my tummy."

6-4

"Grandma won't let go of the dollar till you say,
'Thank you!'"

2-8

"Got some room left in that hug, Mommy?"

9-20

"Oooooh! The wind is ticklin' my tummy!"

*Gayle swinging in the back yard,
1953.*

Gayle's fifth birthday, September 23, 1954.

"Mommy, Jeffy's not singing."

"Whose birthday is next, Mommy?"

Glen's fourth, April 13, 1958.

I drew this cartoon as a tribute to another friend and neighbor in Paradise Valley, Arizona, Sandra Day O'Connor, the first female U.S. Supreme Court Justice. I gave her the original at a dinner in her honor the day it was published. She didn't hand down an opinion on it, but rewarded me with a kiss. Who says there ain't no justice?

"Let's play Supreme Court. You be the old guys and I'll be Sandra Day O'Connor."

EXPRESS LANE
10 ITEMS OR LESS

"Hold it, Mommy! You've got 12 things here!"

DOWSKI

"They're playin' patty-cake."

1-19
Copyright 1974
The Register and Tribune
Syndicate, Inc.

"We're getting our breakfast but we can't find the ice cream scoop."

10-31
Copyright 1972
The Register and Tribune
Syndicate, Inc.

"We're going right back out again as soon as we look at the stuff in our bags."

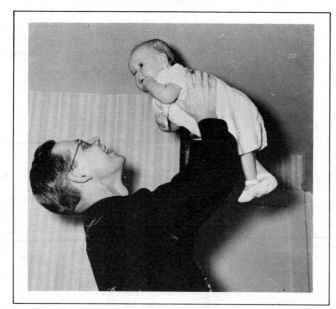

Gayle at four months, January, 1950.

3-6
Copyright 1981
The Register and Tribune
Syndicate, Inc.

"He hasn't been outside today because he has an upset stomach."

Christmas, 1982.

Proof that the years rush by quickly, here is how the Keane clan looked when everybody was home for Christmas in 1982.

However, there is a whole new generation of cartoon idea people waiting to be exploited like their parents were. Three grandchildren, a delight for any grandfather, and a bonanza for a cartoonist!

Claire

Jesse

Max

9-9

Copyright 1978
The Register and Tribune
Syndicate, Inc.

"Why was the commercial so long?"

The original was sent with this inscription: "To Father John Doran who has delivered some of the best commercials I've ever slept through."

4-10

Copyright 1978
The Register and Tribune
Syndicate, Inc.

"That was a long time ago when Mommy was still hidin' PJ under her dress."

7-7

Copyright 1978
The Register and Tribune
Syndicate, Inc.

"It's hot as WHAT out today?"

7-6

"It's okay, Aunt Nancy. You can
have a lick 'cause you're FAMILY."

*In addition to my mother,
other members of my
childhood family show up
in the cartoons. My sister
Nancy, who lives in
Pennsylvania, pays an
occasional visit as Aunt
Nancy and probably wishes
she hadn't.*

11-20

"That's Uncle Bob. He used to be
Daddy's brother."

3-2

"Ah! My bed! My good ol' friendly bed!"

At times I find myself reaching back in my memories to my own childhood for experiences, attitudes, emotions—not gags *per se*, but the basic premise and feelings that I use in constructing a situation involving a child.

Proof that I myself modeled for some of the cartoons I am drawing today is shown in the pictures on these pages. That "horsey" in the snapshot is Al Keane, my father. The front rider is cartoonist Bil Keane at the age of two. My older brother Bob is riding shotgun (1924). He has changed slightly, as shown in the Uncle Bob cartoon on the preceding page.

"Playin' horsey is a NEAT idea, Daddy.
Did you just make it up?"

Romper Room on June 15, 1924, was a daisy field by our home in Crescentville, PA. My bigger brother Bob might have said it (I don't recall): "Boy! Mommy's gonna be RICH!"

6-6

Copyright 1974
The Register and Tribune
Syndicate, Inc.

"Boy! Mommy's gonna be RICH!"

9-18
Copyright 1970
The Register and Tribune
Syndicate, Inc.

"We're playing sailor! Billy's captain, Dolly's cook and I'm first bait!"

CITY OF WILDWOOD LIFE BOAT No. 8

On vacation in New Jersey, 1929. That's our little brother Tom in front of me.

"Why do WE hafta go to bed when Mommy gets tired?"

"...And for all these things we are thankful, Amen. Now, for Christmas I want a bake set, a doll crib, a..."

"I think they're goin' through a phase."

"You're better than just a father. You're a DADDY!"

Family Circus reaches its 25th Anniversary with this
cartoon. Publication date: March 1st, 1985.

One of my biggest thrills came on April 17th, 1983 when I received from the National Cartoonist Society the Reuben Award (named after the designer of the trophy, Rube Goldberg) naming me Cartoonist of the Year for 1982. As President of the Society I held the award dinner for the first time outside New York City. The affair was at the Beverly Hills Hotel in Los Angeles which enabled our entire family to be present for the festivities. Even Billy, Dolly, Jeffy, and PJ rejoiced with me.

That's about all the family snapshots I can put my hands on right now, but if you will stop over to my house tonight I have some home movies of the kids I'd be happy to show for you.

Now that you've met the Keane Clan more intimately and read some of my personal observations I hope you won't quit reading us in the newspaper. Also, as the paperback collections of my cartoons continue to appear be sure to pick them up (better yet, pay for them) and keep in touch.

We love you all.

Now, back to the drawing board for another quarter-century.

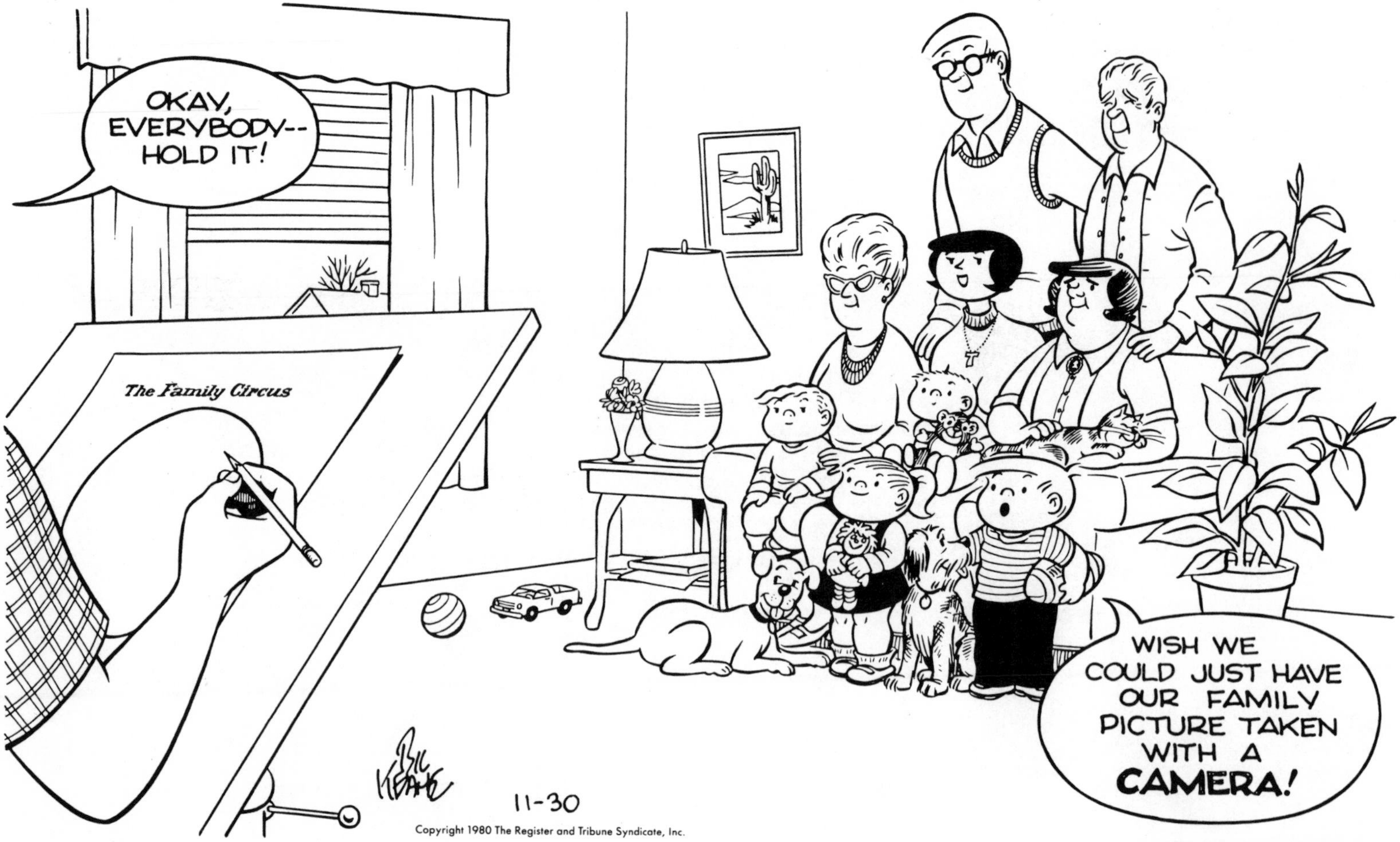
OKAY, EVERYBODY-- HOLD IT!
The Family Circus
WISH WE COULD JUST HAVE OUR FAMILY PICTURE TAKEN WITH A CAMERA!
11-30